The Clarity Series

Community-Based
Learning

The Clarity Series

We face a challenging paradox. Although education is what people and societies have always turned to as a path to a desirable future, the current systems and structures in place actually stand in the way of achieving that preferred state, hindering the true results needed. In this context, educators and students alike are rapidly becoming casualties of an outdated system of education. Given this context, the education community desperately needs an agenda of hope and a *clarity of vision*. Educators feel ongoing tension between what is and what could be in their profession. Many well intended reformers are, in reality, only adding to the initiative fatigue currently plaguing educators. Often educators are finding themselves stuck somewhere between feeling frustrated and being in a state of perpetual paralysis. Sadly, too many educators wonder, in this dynamic landscape, if they really *can* make a difference.

We believe that educators truly can make a difference. Our author team is passionate about leading change, and we have field tested the processes, practices, and innovations that form the basis of the series. Through these volumes, we intend to equip educational leaders with the vision, mindset, skills, and passion for what is possible in public education's future. We will create a new culture where the best and brightest still want to call this profession their own.

The Clarity Series
Community-Based Learning

**Awakening the Mission
of Public Schools**

Holly A. Prast | Donald J. Viegut

CORWIN
A SAGE Company

FOR INFORMATION

Corwin
A SAGE Company
2455 Teller Road
Thousand Oaks, California 91320
www.corwin.com

SAGE Ltd.
1 Oliver's Yard
55 City Road
London, EC1Y 1SP
United Kingdom

SAGE Pvt. Ltd.
B 1/I 1 Mohan Cooperative Industrial Area
Mathura Road, New Delhi 110 044
India

SAGE Publications Asia-Pacific Pte. Ltd.
3 Church Street
#10–04 Samsung Hub
Singapore 049483

Printed in the United States of America

Library of Congress Cataloging-in-Publication Data

A catalog record of this book is available from the Library of Congress.

ISBN: 9781483344515

Acquisitions Editor: Dan Alpert
Associate Editor: Kimberly Greenberg
Editorial Assistant: Cesar Reyes
Project Editor: Veronica Stapleton Hooper
Copy Editor: Amy Rosenstein
Typesetter: Hurix Systems Pvt. Ltd.
Proofreader: Dennis W. Webb
Indexer: Terri Corry
Cover Designer: Janet Kiesel
Marketing Manager: Lisa Lysne

This book is printed on acid-free paper.

Certified Chain of Custody
SUSTAINABLE FORESTRY INITIATIVE
Promoting Sustainable Forestry
www.sfiprogram.org
SFI-01268

SFI label applies to text stock

14 15 16 17 18 10 9 8 7 6 5 4 3 2 1

Contents

List of Figures and Tables   ix

Preface   xi

Acknowledgments   xiii

About the Authors   xvi

1. **An Introduction to Community-Based**
    Learning   **1**
    Increase Student Engagement   2
    Make the Curriculum Relevant and Experiential   2
    Strengthen the Connection Between the
        Community and Schools   3
    The Foundation for Community-Based Learning   5
    Project-Based Learning   5
    Place-Based Learning   5
    Service Learning   6
    The Levels of Community-Based Learning   6
    Community-Based Learning Levels of Partnership   7
    Changing the Work   9

2. **The Foundation for Community-Based**
    Learning   **11**
    Learning Theory   12
    Learning Processes   13
    The Social Nature of Instruction   13
    A Vital Connection   16
    A New Solution to a New Problem   18

3. **A Framework for Community-Based Learning**   **21**
    The CBL Framework   22
    Set the Vision   23
    Create a Common Vocabulary   26
    Plan the Experience   28

	Plan for Sustainability	33
	Implement the Initiative	40
	Assess and Improve	41

4. Case Study: Community-Based Learning School — **49**

	The Beginning of Community-Based Learning School	49
	Making Progress	52
	Challenges Arise	53
	Creating a Curriculum	55
	Setback	56
	Exceeding Expectations	57

5. Essential Practices in Community-Based Learning — **61**

	Drinking the Good Wine First	62
	Get the Right People on the Bus	63
	Source Your Champions	64
	Increase Intentionality	65
	Seek Transfer	66
	Customization and Individualization	66
	Evaluate Current Partnerships	67

6. Professional Development for Community-Based Learning — **71**

	1. Establish Student Learning Goals	72
	2. Determine the Best Practices to Achieve Those Goals	72
	3. Identify the Necessary Resources	75
	4. Decide What Teachers Need to Know and Be Able to Do	77
	5. Gain the Knowledge and Skills	80
	Research	80
	Develop Community Relations Skills	80
	Bring in the Experts	82
	Visit Schools for Examples	82
	Experiment	82
	Reflect and Collaborate	82
	CBL Needs Development	82

7. Leading Community-Based Learning   **85**
Responding to the Need for High Quality   86
A Tolerance for Risk   86
Situational Leadership   88
Distributive Leadership   89
Mindful Leadership   91
Systems Implementation   92

8. Overcoming Barriers   **97**
Time   98
Large-Scale Tests   100
Risk Aversion   100
Partnership Peril   102
Waiting for the Right Time   103
Toxic Leaders   103
Facing Down Detractors   104
Good to Great   105
Existing Structures   105
Wants Over Needs   106

9. Starting Community-Based Learning—Today   **109**
For Teachers   110
For Principals   111
For Superintendents   112
For Boards of Education   113
For Everyone   113

Appendix: Sample Community-Based Learning Unit   **115**
References   **121**
Index   **133**

List of Figures and Tables

Figure 1.1   Community-Based Learning
Levels of Partnership   7

Table 2.1   Common Core/Webb.21st Century Chart   14

Figure 3.1   CBL Framework   23

Figure 3.2   Sample Sociogram   38

Table 3.1   Partnership Tracking Spreadsheet   39

Table 3.2   Educator Rubric   43

Table 3.3   Community Rubric   44

Table 3.4   Student Rubric   45

Table 5.1   Benchmark Log   68

Table 5.2   Partnership Assessment Tool   69

Preface

$\mathcal{D}$id you know that the United Way was originally started by five people? Five well-intended people saw the need for citizens to get together to address their community needs. They collaborated around a common vision of health and education, and more than 125 years later, the United Way is present in more than 45 countries and territories around the world, growing and sustaining that work. Whether or not the United Way inspires you to action, the concept of starting off small and growing into something much bigger is a common story in our culture. This book asks readers to consider how their individual action could lead to a radical change in the way we approach education today.

Community-based learning is an educational strategy. Community-based learning calls educators to invite the community into their classroom, but not in the typical "guest lecture" fashion. Instead, educators are asked to involve the community member in the planning of the curriculum so that the educational experiences can be connected to the work that is happening in the community.

Imagine a math lesson that asks students to use fractions. Think of the businesses and organizations in your community that apply this knowledge every day! What if you brought in the owner of a small gift shop and asked her help in teaching fractions? Students might end up pricing various items and figuring out the tipping point for profit through markdowns. Not only would this be an engaging lesson for a variety of reasons, but in the end, the educator and the community business owner would have built a powerful connection.

ABOUT THIS BOOK

In this day and age, when curriculum needs to be more relevant and community support for schools is fragile, community-based learning offers educators a way to address both challenges with one solution. This book was written to help educators understand and ultimately be able to replicate the practice of community-based learning. Chapters 1 and 2 give an overview and rationale for the practice. Chapter 3 establishes the framework for systemic implementation of the practice. Chapter 4 goes in-depth with a case study of a school that implemented the practice on a moderate scale, with 75 high school students. Chapters 5 and 6 analyze important instructional and leadership practices, while Chapter 7 addresses common barriers to the implementation of the practice. Those in leadership positions will find helpful strategies in Chapter 8, and Chapter 9 gives educators ideas for taking that "first step."

Each chapter includes examples from around the world where similar practices are taking place. The chapters also include questions for your reflection. For community-based learning to be successful, it must align to your mission, vision, and goals. These questions were designed to help you take the concepts presented and explore the possibilities within your own setting.

Many books on school-community relations will explain the importance of stakeholder involvement. Those types of books help the reader who is interested in understanding traditional school-community relationships. This book is intended to give readers a practical, how-to guide to an innovative approach for building a strong community bond while deepening learning experiences. For those needing to do both, community-based learning is a concept worth investigating.

"One" is a very powerful number. *Community-Based Learning: Awakening the Mission of Public Schools* gives you the tools to initiate change from a single classroom. You, as a single educator, have the ability to engage in an instructional strategy that can potentially positively impact the entire system, from your students to the community in which you educate. The changes in the education world grow with each year. How will you rise to the challenge and be that educator who finds innovative solutions to the increasing challenges? Community-based learning is a great place to start.

Acknowledgments

*D*an Alpert: Your expertise and guidance has been invaluable. Thank you for believing in us from the start.

Valerie von Frank: You are quite simply amazing. Your talent and critical feedback made us better every step of the way.

The Clarity authors—Dr. Pat Greco, Dr. Karen Wendorf-Heldt, Dr. Mary Gavigan, Dr. Tony Frontier, and soon-to-be Dr. Kim Brown: What a fantastic team! We are proud to call ourselves colleagues and friends.

Julie Dumke, Rick Leib, Oliver Schinkten, and Brad Weber: You are the most dedicated and outstanding group of educators with whom I have had the privilege of working. Thank you for your dedication to the dream and making sure that it lives on.

Jami Kohl: Your courage as a leader and creative implementation of CBL allowed the practice to be raised to an entirely new level. For all of this, and for organizing the most engaging and thoughtful board presentation in history, we offer you our gratitude!

Dr. Andrew Jones: You took a chance on an idea that yielded unbelievable results. Thank you for your unwavering support and strict attention to accountability.

Dr. David Gundlach: A person could not ask for a better wingman. Thank you for being there exactly when it counted.

Dr. Janice Jones: Thank you for your flexibility and willingness to merge research and application as acceptable practice.

Reuben Jacobson: Carry on with the vision! You are an inspiration and a person we are fortunate to be able to call a colleague.

Jamie Vollmer: So often those who find notoriety in their work are inaccessible to those starting out. Thank you for not being that person. Our conversation early on in the work changed everything.

Bob Tess: Your loyalty and bravery are inspiring. For a man who doesn't like transition, you certainly seem to flourish in the face of it.

Dr. Donald Viegut: You took a chance, probably before I was ready. You have a talent for bringing the best out of people. I appreciate you in every aspect—as a mentor, colleague, and friend.

Dr. Carroll Bronson: Brains and beauty are not mutually exclusive. You are beautiful inside and out, and your guidance as a woman and an academic have been invaluable.

Dr. Peter Jonas: Thank you for knowing exactly how to pick up the pieces, say the right thing, keep me on track, and push me when I needed pushing. Your humor, common sense, and efficiency made you the perfect chair for me. And I know—you don't care if I have to work hard!

Dr. Robert Mayfield: You have this uncanny ability to clearly set expectations and do everything necessary to keep people on track toward that vision while giving them a sense of complete autonomy. It is a gift. The people who work with you admire and respect you more every day. When I took this job, I told the board I wanted to spend time learning from a great leader, I just didn't know if it was you. It is.

Mary and Don Terrien: How do you even add up the hours of support you have given me? Without the two of you, this would never have been possible. Thank you for all of the time and patience. I'm back!

Cameron and Laurene Rottier; Alexandra and Nathaniel Prast: For all the times when I was present without truly being present. For all of the games and concerts I had to miss. For all of the times I couldn't be a mom. Thank you for understanding and loving me anyway. I love you all!

The Prast Family: There was never a question that I was a Prast. Long before I officially entered the family, you treated me as one of your own. I am forever grateful.

Cohort 22: You have each left a handprint on my heart that has changed me forever.

Vibe 22: Hit it and quit it! 'Nough said.

Jeremiah (JJ) Arnold: A friend like no other. Thank you for not letting me quit and believing in me even in the darker moments. I will cherish our friendship for life.

Dr. Derek Matthews: You have taught me to expect the unexpected and to live the story.

Peggy Black: You are an inspiration to me in so many ways: as a mom, a woman, an educator, a businesswoman, a confidant, and a person. I am blessed by our friendship.

Kim Brown: What do you even say to a person who has lived this journey the way we have? I could not have done it without you. You see the good in everyone, and you have more faith in me than I do in myself. For that and so much more I will always be in debt to you, my twin.

James Prast: For most of my life I lived in fear of failing. You have taught me so much. In this crazy three-year academic journey, you were there to remind me that failure is an opportunity for growth and part of the road to success. You believed in me when I lost hope. You got me back on track by never accepting my self-doubt as truth. And you knew when I needed to simply stop and have popcorn and beer. You make me a better person and I love you with all my heart.

PUBLISHER'S ACKNOWLEDGMENTS

Corwin gratefully acknowledges the contributions of the following reviewers:

Sandra Dop

Consultant, 21st Century Skills

Iowa Department of Education

Howard W. Smith

Superintendent of Schools

Public Schools of the Tarrytowns

Sleepy Hollow, NY

About the Authors

 **Holly A. Prast,** PhD, received her doctoral degree in Leadership for the Advancement of Learning and Service from Cardinal Stritch University. She has 18 years of experience in private and public educational settings, with 4 years in teaching and 14 in administration. Holly has served as a building principal, and at the district office level in assessment, school improvement, English as a second language, strategic planning, community engagement, director of administration, and currently holds the position of assistant superintendent in a district in the state of Wisconsin. Holly has also served on the graduate advisory board for Silver Lake College. Holly has spoken nationally and in her home state of Wisconsin on the community-based learning approach to education. Holly is a proud wife and mother of four teenagers.

Dr. Donald J. Viegut has served as a classroom teacher, building principal, director of curriculum, deputy superintendent, and superintendent and currently serves as agency administrator of a regional service delivery agency. Don has served as president of Wisconsin ASCD and served on the Board of Directors for ASCD, and Chair of the Board of North Central Technical College. Don also served as the chair of the preK–18 Council for the University of Wisconsin-Steven's Point. Don coauthored *Common Formative Assessments*, a million-dollar Corwin publication. Don has presented nationally and networked extensively throughout the world. Don earned his doctorate from Western Michigan University.

We would like to dedicate this book to our families, especially Jim and Judy. You have been with us every step of the way, and endured all of the ups and downs. Your support has meant everything and made this endeavor possible.

And to all of the educators who have shared their community-based learning experiences with us. Your contributions have made this work better and stronger. We are so fortunate to have been a part of your journey.

CHAPTER 1

An Introduction to Community– Based Learning

Schools cannot do it alone.

—Jamie Vollmer (2010)

MAIN IDEA

Authentic community-based learning results in:

- Collaboration between educators and partners

- Improved understanding of each other's setting

- Increased relevance of the curriculum for students, who learn through problem-based instruction

---

At the 2013 Association for Supervision and Curriculum Development (ASCD) conference in Chicago, Illinois, a teacher lamented about changes in education. "We can't do it all anymore," the teacher said. "There is so much we need to tend to for our kids, and we can't keep all the plates in the air." Educators are asked to perform an incredible feat. They must teach content, mind the needs of the whole child (ASCD, 2012), and prepare students for college or career. They also must know how to collect, analyze, and interpret data to make decisions to achieve all these goals. The time and energy required to meet individualized student needs has become overwhelming. With the Common Core State Standards and related assessments challenging the level of instruction students are receiving, educators are more eager than ever to know what works.

How can we as educators begin to think differently about how we educate young people? How can we address higher-order skills to better prepare students without overwhelming them and causing them to lose sight of what is truly important? And how can we meet the rapid pace of change required in education today? The answer is for each of us to find innovative and strategic solutions.

One such solution is community-based learning (CBL). While many changes called for in schools today are systemic and complex, a single educator can establish CBL and make a significant difference in a classroom, school, and community. CBL is an educational strategy that one educator can use to:

- Increase student engagement
- Make the curriculum relevant and experiential
- Strengthen the connection between the community and schools

INCREASE STUDENT ENGAGEMENT

Phil Schlechty (2011), educational researcher and founder of the Schlechty Center, identified criteria for determining true student engagement: personal meaning, persistence, belief in ability to accomplish, and high quality. These indicators of true engagement are evident when CBL is practiced successfully.

MAKE THE CURRICULUM RELEVANT AND EXPERIENTIAL

David Kolb (1984) breaks down experiential learning into four categories: (1) concrete experience (the student does something),

(2) reflective observation (the student thinks about what he or she has done), (3) abstract conceptualization (the student creates a new idea from the experience), and (4) active experimentation (the student tries out his or her version of the experience). CBL is a strategy grounded in student experiences. Community partners live in the experiential world every day, applying their knowledge to their craft. By having those partners in the classroom working with educators, students have the opportunity to see knowledge applied beyond the classroom. Students also experience application when they take part in projects that connect to the world outside their classroom.

For example, a student may work with a local farmer to plant, cultivate, harvest, and sell a garden of food. The teacher can work to align curricular benchmarks to that experience (i.e., profit margins from sales). This gives the student a concrete experience. Given the opportunity to reflect, that student will be able to think about what he or she has done and the impact it has on the student's learning and the community (reflective observation). That student might then create a new way to apply profit margins to something else (abstract conceptualization). Eventually, the hope is that the student will make meaning of the concept and try out this experience in a new setting (active experimentation). CBL allows educators to maximize experiences like these through curricular connections in and out of the classroom.

STRENGTHEN THE CONNECTION BETWEEN THE COMMUNITY AND SCHOOLS

Why do people become disgruntled with public schools and the students who are products of the system? "People don't leave public schools because they aren't involved," according to Jamie Vollmer, a businessman turned educational advocate who has dedicated the last 25 years to bridging the gap between communities and schools. "They aren't involved because they leave public schools" (personal communication, 2011).

CBL begins to outline a solution to the problems between schools and communities:

- Communities often are too distant from the schools that exist within them.

- Many of those outside of education do not understand educators, and educators sometimes do not understand the perspective of those outside of education. CBL allows educators to work smarter by marrying best practice and advocacy.

Most educators are familiar with the rhetoric: *Students aren't prepared. Kids today don't value hard work. Students in other countries are outperforming U.S. students.* To change the status quo in the face of these perceptions and debunk the stereotypes, schools need to reengage their communities.

The proliferation of technology makes it seem that people have more information, but knowing more does not always translate to being more connected. Community members may find out what is *happening* in schools, but may not have relationships with the schools. Schools may have numerous partnerships, ranging from superficial to deep, but may not be maximizing partnership possibilities to create a stronger overall community.

INCREASING ENGAGEMENT FOR STUDENTS

In Hartford, Connecticut, students spent a year researching a topic relevant for them—binge drinking. As with students in many communities around the United States, binge drinking was seen as the norm in Hartford. The students set out to dispel that idea, and at the same time, to develop their research and problem-solving skills. "Through surveys and in-depth interviews the group was able to learn about the scenarios and circumstances in which their peers engage in binge drinking," according to Communications Coordinator Connie Yan (2003). The Institute for Community Research, a community organization, collaborated with the students from Conard and Hall High Schools on their research in a year-long research study on the binge drinking behaviors of their peers (Yan, 2003). Finally, students worked with a local theater troupe (Hartbeat Ensemble) to develop plays based on their findings.

Approximately 2,000 miles across the country, Manor New Tech High School in Texas is being heralded for its innovative ways of engaging students. "Bored students are not engaged students, so at Manor New Tech, teachers don't lecture," writes Kelsey Sheehy, an education reporter for *U.S. News and World Report* (2013). New Tech has transitioned to all project-based learning to engage students and

(Continued)

prepare them for life after K–12 education. Students direct their own learning and explore problems rather than waiting for teachers to present them with the material. The school is among only about 1% of schools nationwide that use a project-based learning instructional model (Merrow, 2013). New Tech has received national attention for the innovation, and its students have improved their attendance, graduation, and college acceptance rates (Texas Education Agency, 2013).

CBL Link: Successful educators employ strategies such as CBL to increase student engagement, achievement, and mastery of 21st century skills. When students find meaning in what they are learning, they are more passionate about the subject matter and achieve more (Kolb, 1984).

THE FOUNDATION FOR COMMUNITY-BASED LEARNING

CBL has its roots in three strategies—project-based learning, place-based learning, and service learning. To understand CBL, it is important to understand the bases for these strategies.

Project-Based Learning

Project-based learning focuses on the understanding that for students to be more engaged, they need to make meaning of the content they are studying, not just acquire it (Wiggins & McTighe, 2011). Educators arrange learning experiences so students can look at the larger questions in a unit rather than looking incrementally at disconnected pieces. Students tackle a "project" and through that project achieve benchmarks and retain what they have learned (Buck Institute for Education, 2013).

Place-Based Learning

The underlying theory of place-based learning is that students will understand how content is relevant and can be applied if they see it in a real-world setting. When students engage in place-based learning, they get out of the classroom and go to where the learning is being used. These authentic learning experiences are the basis for the Common Core State Standards. Educators are asked to help students see how what they know and understand can be transferred to real-world applications (Center for Ecoliteracy, 2013).

Service Learning

Students who are part of service learning see how their actions can change the world. The goal of service learning is to help students become active and contributing citizens, connecting them to their community. Education is designed so that students learn through opportunities that allow them to give back and serve the local, state, national, and global communities in which they live (National Service Learning Clearinghouse, 2013).

CBL combines components of project-based learning, place-based learning, and service learning and adds the expectations of engaged students, a dynamic curriculum, and a connected community. None of the three foundational strategies address all three factors that CBL does: student engagement, a relevant, experiential curriculum, and community engagement. Project-based learning, place-based learning, and service learning address one or two core components but do not complete the trifecta in learning.

CBL asks teachers to seek out and work with community members to plan relevant lessons that address curricular needs. If educators do this well, community members know more about the school through their involvement. Teachers multiply their effectiveness as educators. And when students see their work making a difference, they become more passionate about learning.

THE LEVELS OF COMMUNITY-BASED LEARNING

Many educators report that they already do CBL, but few engage in authentic practice. While educators are familiar with the concept of engaging stakeholders, they often pay attention only to stakeholders that they identify as important (Freeman, 2010). The CBL levels-of-partnership pyramid in Figure 1.1 helps delineate the concept of CBL from other partnerships that may exist within a school or district.

Community–Based Learning Levels of Partnership

The first level in the pyramid is a pre-partnership stage called information. In this stage, schools and the community know that the other exists, and that is about the extent of the relationship. For example, a person might drive by a business every day. He might say to himself, "Oh, right! I know where that is. I drive by it on my way to work." He is informed of that organization's existence. It's not much of a partnership, but it is a place to start.

The second level on the continuum, communication, occurs when the two entities begin to talk to one another. The school promotes a community event, for example, or the business puts up a flyer to help promote a school event.

In level three—the relationship stage—the school and partner work with one another, but their activities are unconnected to curriculum or instruction. The school might send the choir to sing

Figure 1.1   Community-Based Learning Levels of Partnership

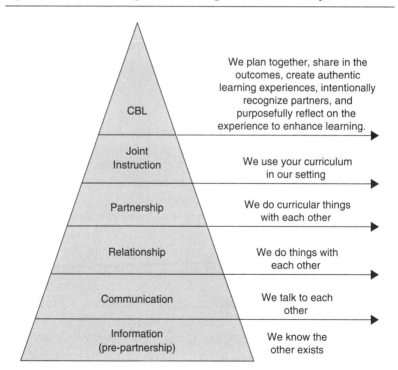

for a local business event, for example, or a local bookstore might donate books to the school. Neither activity has inherent curricular meaning, but the activity is the beginning of a more purposeful relationship between community and school.

True partnerships begin at the fourth level, the first stage of potential *curricular* partnerships. At the partnership level, educators engage in activities that create curricular connections. For example, the reading teacher works to meet literacy benchmarks when students create a repertoire of songs they will sing at a business event, or the science teacher aligns a lesson plan to science standards and has students write an essay for the local energy company's contest.

At level five, joint instruction, educators have clear curricular goals but do not join with the partner to plan curriculum. In the joint instruction phase, partners allow their settings to be used to enhance the curriculum, such as with programs including Drug Abuse Resistance Education (DARE; Miller & Parsons, 2010). Law enforcement created the DARE curriculum, and schools allow it to be taught during the school day. Conversely, educators often plan curricula and then go into the field to allow students to apply what they learn. For instance, in a unit on local government, teachers might take students to the state legislature to witness government in action.

At the highest level of partnership—the level of true CBL—partners:

- **Collaboratively plan curriculum.** When people work together, they understand expected outcomes, work together to achieve them, can use resources more efficiently, and lessen the unpredictability of trying a new innovation (Jennings & Mamdani, 1992).
- **Improve understanding of each other's setting.** When educators restrict teaching and learning to what occurs within school walls, they live in an echo chamber. By working in the world beyond school, they appreciate the rich learning opportunities that exist in the community and gain a sharper understanding of 21st century workplace needs. They then become advocates for non-school-based experiences. The reverse is also true. When community partners experience the effort that goes into planning a

high-quality curricular experience for students, they better appreciate the complexities of the teaching–learning process. They learn that teaching requires more than seven hours a day with summers off.

- **Increase relevance for those involved.** Students gain richer learning experiences that heighten their desire to learn (International Center for Leadership in Education, n.d.). Teachers are better able to meet the Common Core State Standards by creating learning experiences that facilitate higher-order thinking. Community partners share expertise to help cultivate and activate young citizens.

CHANGING THE WORK

Educators are facing initiative fatigue. Vollmer (2010) traced the history of the expectations placed upon educators since 1900 and compiled a list of "the ever increasing burden on America's public schools" (p. 30). Vollmer points out that society continues to add expectations without adding time or resources.

The educator's work today is daunting: screening all students, meeting testing requirements in the era of high-stakes accountability, monitoring individual student progress, teaching 21st century skills, meeting newly adopted Common Core State Standards, designing and implementing interventions for students not meeting the standards, differentiating instruction to match individual student needs, continually modifying instruction, scaffolding learning, accommodating special needs, teaching high-level core content, working with students on soft skills, providing enrichment courses, working with the whole child—and the list goes on.

With all that is asked of educators today, how can they do something *else?* Great educators understand that performing all these tasks requires reframing them so that educating students becomes a manageable endeavor. CBL can help educators manage all these expectations by customizing learning.

At first, CBL can feel like another "thing" added to the list, but once educators understand and practice it, they see that the strategy is designed to streamline their work. CBL replaces rather than adds to direct instruction.

Questions for Reflection

1. In our district, what factors are causing *more* but not necessarily *better* work for educators? What are the factors in our district that are causing educators the most stress?

2. How does the structure of CBL address some of these factors?

3. How has our district addressed the components of the Common Core State Standards that call for increased relevance and real-world experience for students?

4. How well does our community understand and support the unique challenges of our educational setting?

CHAPTER 2

The Foundation for Community– Based Learning

MAIN IDEA

Community-based learning has its foundation in research-based experiential learning practices and can benefit not only students, but those outside of schools by strengthening the community.

Simon Sinek (2009) is probably most famous for what he calls his "golden circle," the notion that successful ideas begin when innovators can answer *why*. Sinek represents the idea by drawing a circle that looks like a target and writing the word *why* in the center.

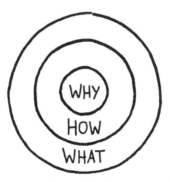

Source: Sinek (2009), www.ted.com/talks/simon_sinek_how_great_leaders_ inspire_action.html. Used with permission.

"People don't buy what you do, they buy *why* you do it," Sinek says ("Simon Sinek: How Great Leaders Inspire Action," 2009). To begin community-based learning (CBL), it's important to be able to explain why.

LEARNING THEORY

Schools are at a precipice with the Common Core State Standards. The new requirements are forcing changes in instructional practices. The Common Core State Standards state: "The standards are designed to be robust and relevant to the real world, reflecting the knowledge and skills that our young people need for success in college and careers" (Common Core State Standards Initiative, 2013). To realize the standards' full instructional potential, teachers need to help students better understand relevance and think more critically.

Experiential learning theory (Kolb, 1984) tells us that experiences help students connect curriculum and application, allowing them to become more engaged in their learning. When students are engaged, their achievement improves (Carini, Kuh, & Klein, in press).

Educational research supports an authentic approach to learning that is the cornerstone of CBL. Kolb's (1984) experiential learning theory, Flavell's theory of metacognition (1979), and the work of Lewin (1947), Dewey (1938), and Piaget (1954) support the idea that authentic learning activities need to connect to experiences that are meaningful to students. Does memorization of facts do that? Most of us would say no.

Institutions of higher education (IHEs) have historically given students real-world, relevant learning experiences to better prepare them to enter the workforce. In 2006, students from California State University, Fullerton, worked with Target stores to create an authentic learning experience for the students in the College of Business and Economics and the College of Communication. Target wanted to find future leaders (Brzovic & Matz, 2009, p. 22). The Fullerton students assessed the organization and made recommendations, not only helping solve a major company's issue, but honing their problem-solving, collaboration, and communication skills. As a result, they were better able to connect their classroom learning to real-world implications.

Students completed this work while becoming active community members. Professional preparation programs from teaching to medicine to engineering to health and human services traditionally provide rich, real-world experiences, begging the question, Why is experiential learning limited primarily to postsecondary education? What in our beliefs, structures, and leadership keeps public educators from teaching experientially from the moment students enter school?

LEARNING PROCESSES

Norman L. Webb (2002), senior researcher with the Wisconsin Center for Educational Research, developed a Depth of Knowledge Scale grounded in Benjamin Bloom's taxonomy. Webb organizes learning processes into four levels: recall, skill/concept, strategic thinking, and extended thinking.

Webb identifies and compares levels of knowledge that are present in current educational structures and challenges educators to scaffold learning activities and assessments so that they are consistent, aligned, and logical. Webb also emphasizes being intentional when planning learning experiences and assessments at each level. Comparing the Common Core State Standards, the 21st century skills outlined in the 21st century skills framework (Partnership for 21st Century Skills, 2011), and Webb's Depth of Knowledge Scale reveals commonalities (see Table 2.1, Common Core/Webb.21st Century Chart).

Each set of standards expects students to engage in deep learning through authentic experiences that emphasize communication, collaboration, and problem solving. Robert Marzano (2012) says that "using cooperative learning helps teachers lay the foundation for student success in a world that depends on collaboration and cooperation" (p. 37). Such higher level learning experiences are a vital part of CBL.

THE SOCIAL NATURE OF INSTRUCTION

In 1995 in Massachusetts, Heidi and Phil Jackson gave birth to twin girls they named Kyrie and Brielle. Both girls were premature and underweight. While Kyrie did well, Brielle declined until a nurse caring for the girls had an idea. She placed healthy Kyrie in the incubator with Brielle. A photograph shows the moment Kyrie

Table 2.1   Common Core/Webb.21st Century Chart

Common Core State Standards	Level Four of Webb's Depth of Knowledge (Extend Strategic Thinking)	21st Century Standards
"The standards are designed to be robust and relevant to the real world, reflecting the knowledge and skills that our young people need for success in college and careers."	"Students are engaged in conducting investigations to solve real-world problems with unpredictable outcomes."	"Engages student with the real-world data, tools, and experts they will encounter in college, on the job, and in life—students learn best when actively engaged in solving meaningful problems."
http://www.corestandards.org/	http://www.aps.edu/rda/documents/resources/Webbs_DOK_Guide.pdf	http://www.p21.org/about-us/p21-framework/351-21st-century-standards

put her arm around her ailing sister and the healing began. Brielle's heart rate and color improved, and with her sister by her side, she eventually was healthy enough to go home (Jackson, 2001).

Humans need to be social. Michael Dickmann and Nancy Stanford-Blair (2009) identify "social nature" as one of the brain's six core constructs (along with the physiological, emotional, constructive, reflective, and dispositional natures). Dickmann and Stanford-Blair outline humans' biological need to interact socially and explain that humans learn better when exposed to others. Some might argue that social learning is achieved in a regular classroom through interactions with peers, and that may be true when collaborative learning is constructed appropriately. However, learning is enhanced when the learning itself is social (Dickmann & Stanford-Blair, 2009). Paired with the experiential/constructivist learning that is the foundation of CBL, students learn better when the learning is relevant and accomplished collaboratively.

Jane David (2008) researched project-based learning and concludes that "using real-life problems to motivate students, challenging them to think deeply about meaningful content, and enabling them to work collaboratively are practices that yield benefits for all students" (p. 82).

CBL centers on the idea of a larger community as essential to learning. Community is manifested in three ways:

- Students learn better in social situations and when they know their work is relevant (Dickmann & Stanford-Blair, 2009).
- By planning and instructing in a collaborative (social) manner, educators maximize the capacity of numerous bodies of knowledge and experience.
- When community leaders go beyond the doors of their own organization to socialize with the broader community, they enrich their community and the organization they represent.

John Hattie's meta-analysis (2009) identifies a number of effective educational practices. Hattie states that students need to work together rather than in isolation. "Both cooperative and competitive learning are more effective than individualistic methods—pointing again to the power of peers in the learning equation," he writes (p. 212).

Dean, Hubbell, Pitler, and Stone (2012) point out that students learn better, find deeper meaning in the material, and are more engaged when they work together. Though this research is relatively recent, the idea of socialization as a critical component in learning appeared earlier in educational theory. Lev Vygotsky (1988) believed that cognition was inseparably linked to socialization. "The essence of the child's mental development lies in the progressive socialization of the child's thought," he writes (p. 174). John Dewey (1938) set the foundations for this social construct when he said common experiences affect individual learning. Research supports that students learn better when they are together—because they are more engaged in the experience.

MEANINGFUL CONNECTIONS

The social nature of instruction in CBL involves not only students working with other students, but the potential of students working to achieve a goal for their community.

In a regular high school graphic arts class, students might select a project to work on throughout the semester and produce a culminating project, such as a logo. A Wisconsin class engaging in CBL had each

(Continued)

(Continued)

group of students work on a T-shirt design for a local organization. Some were for nonprofit organizations, others for baseball teams local businesses sponsored, and some were for school clubs. Students knew their end product was meaningful. People would wear their design, and the students might see their logos as they walked down the street or shopped in their community. The design was the target benchmark, but additional benchmarks abounded: Students had to consistently communicate with clients to ensure the design was satisfactory. They had to collaborate with others in their group so that all members understood and embraced their roles and responsibilities for the project. Some students researched a company's existing designs and that of similar companies to ensure that they did not stray too far from the organization's image or brand. To reap the benefits of this learning experience, students couldn't perform the task alone.

A VITAL CONNECTION

In the late 1990s, many schools explored a shift from "drill and kill" math texts to more engaging problem solving—teaching students to use a metacognitive approach and think about the thinking. Educators who made this switch without educating the public and involving stakeholders in selecting the new texts generated friction and controversy. Conversely, many districts made a smooth transition into this new method of instruction when district leaders took the time to educate the public on the switch to a new program, to involve them in the process, and to help them understand the reasoning behind the change. The change in math illustrates how communities support or detract from what is best for students based on stakeholders' understanding of the issue.

CBL can help build much-needed bridges to stakeholders who oftentimes are critical of public education. Calls for public education to be more responsive, adaptable, and flexible are being heard on every front (McCaffrey, 2013; Richards, Brown, & Forde, 2006; Young, 1990). Whether that need is real or perceived, any entity viewed as the big ship that can't be turned should be concerned. Critics charge that public education isn't changing or improving (Carvallo & Paine, 2011; Klein, 2011; Layton, 2013; Stein,

2010). The problem is that society is changing faster than the public schools (McNulty, 2011).

Jamie Vollmer businessman and education advocate, analyzed the historical plight of public education, tracing initiative implementation from the 1800s to the present. According to Vollmer, "We have raised the bar from requiring universal student *attendance* to demanding universal student *achievement*. No generation of educators in the history of the world has been asked to accomplish this goal" (pp. 52–53). He states that major changes in the system are needed to help students learn instead of just get through, pointing out that students' road to change is through the community. "[Community] understanding, trust, permission, and support," he writes. "This is what we need to make changes and make them stick. Armed with these four, we dramatically increase our chances of creating schools that unfold the potential of every child" (Vollmer, 2010, p. 117). Through CBL, educators help community members understand the quality of education today and learn how schools are improving through curricular benchmarks. Community members help educators find relevance for the students and community. Students solve problems and learn strategies that equip them to be college and career ready and ultimately improve the communities in which they live. When educators resist the temptation to be satisfied with excellent instructional practices alone, and create CBL, they break down traditional barriers between schools and community. The potential then exists not only to increase students' depth of knowledge and the face of education, but also to change communities.

Stein Rogan and Partners (2008) found that schools are disconnected from their communities. The study states that more than half of sampled districts did not "have a strategic solution for connecting to their communities" (p. 3). CBL allows educators to tackle instructional best practice, capitalize on the experts in the field, and connect to the community. Designing deep, authentic learning experiences that don't link back to the community misses a golden opportunity for educators to strengthen communities' relationships with schools. At the same time, students are more engaged, prepared for college, 21st century careers, and are better equipped to become lifelong learners.

THE SUCCESS OF PLACE–BASED LEARNING

Place-based learning is one of the instructional methods closely related to CBL. In *Place-Based Education: Connecting Classrooms & Communities* (2005), David Sobel offers empirical and anecdotal evidence of the success of place-based learning nationwide. Sobel, director of certification programs in the Department of Education at Antioch University in New England, writes of students in a Littleton, New Hampshire, school:

> The town is already functioning as a classroom in a novel collaboration between Chutter's General Store and the marketing program at the Littleton High School's vocational center. When the well-established downtown candy store realized that its Internet sales site was costing more than the revenues it generated, the owners looked to the school for a solution. The high school needed more space and the marketing class was seeking real-world projects. The school district and the town agreed to rehabilitate a space below the candy store to create a marketing classroom for less than it would cost to build new space at the high school. By having the marketing class take over Chutter's Internet business, the students get economics experience and the candy store owners generate a bit of revenue as a result of the reduced labor costs. Through a balanced focus on economic development and environmental preservation, the community gets revitalized and the state curriculum standards are met. (Sobel, 2005, p. 2)

A NEW SOLUTION TO A NEW PROBLEM

David Mathews (1996), a former U.S. Secretary of Health, Education, and Welfare, writes that schools have lost track of their original mission. Others contend that the mission of schooling has changed. Vollmer (2010) says that education's purpose has remained the same since public schooling began in the mid-1600s—to meet the needs of the community. What *has* changed is the definition of a community. In the days of the one-room schoolhouse, communities were self-contained entities. Blacksmiths, carpenters, farmers, and teachers were necessary to sustain the community.

Today, students' community is the world. School buildings, located in neighborhoods, are linked to an interconnected network through which vast amounts of information can be acquired and communicated in seconds. Educators now are charged with the task of customizing teaching and learning to prepare students for a world of unforeseen possibilities (Darling-Hammond, 2010). Educators suddenly need to customize the educational experience for an entire world of possibilities.

Content acquisition, the primary goal of the educational system throughout the 19th and 20th centuries, is no longer sufficient to prepare students for future challenges. Education cannot consist of content acquisition alone. Students need learning experiences that allow them to make meaning and to deepen their understanding by using what they have learned (Common Core State Standards Initiative, 2013).

Educators seeking a means to improve their craft and students' experience can use the curriculum as a foundation and the community as the cornerstone rather than a backdrop. The tools and strategies of CBL can help teachers raise the bar to meet the Common Core standards without adding on to their current work. CBL simply requires teachers to teach differently.

Questions for Reflection

1. What are some of the most memorable moments in my educational career? Did these moments involve content acquisition or applying that content to something more meaningful?
2. How do students learn differently when learning is related to experiences that have relevance for them and the community?
3. How would our school and district benefit from a more involved relationship with members of our community?

CHAPTER 3

A Framework for Community-Based Learning

MAIN IDEA

Community-based learning combines best instructional practices with community expertise to bring about change that makes a difference.

Teachers have been trained to teach a subject, but they seldom apply content to work in a field. Community members work with content knowledge in practical ways every day, yet they seldom pass on their experience unless they are succession planning. Marshall Goldsmith, Cathy Greenberg, Alastair Robertson, and Maya Hu-Chan (2003) call the "model of the future" a collaboration that relies on "collective responsibility and accountability" (p. 4).

In community-based learning (CBL), a common agenda is essential. Teachers and community members each want what is best for students. Both have a vested interest and their own approach to helping students achieve their potential.

Understanding that no one person has expertise in all areas, it makes sense to work together.

As David Orentlicher, author of *Two Presidents Are Better Than One: The Case for a Bipartisan Executive Branch*, contends, the more people who are involved in making a decision, the more representative the decision will be of a common rather than partisan agenda. Orentlicher in fact proposed a co-presidency to expand representation in government. He says decisions are best made by at least two and up to 50 people (Mertens, Cherry, & Taylor, 2010). CBL combines best instructional practices with community members' expertise.

Many approaches to improving education often require large-scale implementation and complex systems thinking. While the ultimate goal is large-scale implementation of CBL, the effort needed to attain that level requires intensive time and energy. Planning a single CBL experience is more easily achieved. Any educator—a teacher, a principal, or a district leader—has the ability to work with a partner to create a CBL experience. The following framework is intended to assist educators in creating a CBL experience.

THE CBL FRAMEWORK

The framework for CBL isn't new, but its application to CBL is. The framework comprises these steps:

1. Set the vision

2. Create common vocabulary

3. Plan the experience

4. Plan for sustainability

5. Implement

6. Assess and improve

Figure 3.1, the CBL Framework, shows the progression of this framework, adapted from Melaville, Jacobson, and Blank (2011). The pinnacle of the experience—the desired outcome— is expressed in the vision. A common vocabulary then runs

Figure 3.1　CBL Framework

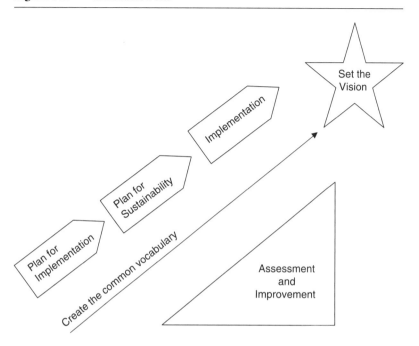

throughout the process to provide clarity for those involved in the process. The designers plan the experience and move from planning implementation to planning for sustainability, and finally to implementing the learning experience. Throughout the process, designers assess the effort and reflect on the practice in order to continuously improve the experience. Each section scales up the effort (Melaville et al., 2011).

Set the Vision

One month into one district's flagship CBL experience, CBL team members and their spouses went to dinner to celebrate the learning project's successes. As teachers reminisced about their summer spent planning the year's events, they recalled the long days away from families. Their spouses, who were along for the evening, assumed that the dinner was to celebrate the completion of the work, but later that evening, one teacher said, "We really need to get together now and plan the curriculum for the second unit." His wife's jaw dropped, and without thinking she said, "What were you *doing* all summer long?"

These teachers had been working hard, but they didn't have a lot on paper to show for it. The first step to successful systemic implementation is setting a vision and effectively communicating it (Sheppard & Brown, 2009). The teacher's wife didn't understand the necessity of developing a philosophy. Team members first had to understand their beliefs. They then had to do the important work of creating a mission, vision, and philosophy based on those beliefs so that their work was grounded. They had researched successful examples of CBL, developed their understanding of the community, mapped the district dynamics, and organized tasks. Unit planning was one piece of the conversation, and the curriculum was evolving. They had spent a great deal of time carefully framing their vision and aligning their philosophy to the vision.

Creating a vision requires examining the organization's beliefs. Once they have been identified, those beliefs are then aligned to the needs of the district and its community. From there, organizers develop goals and action steps so that all members of the educational community understand where they are currently and what they need to do to get where they want to be. For example, a district might believe that schools are organizations integral to the community. Given that belief, the district may identify the need for shared outcomes between community and school. From there, planners might develop a goal of developing a collaborative planning process between community and school. A resulting action step might be establishing curricular school-community partnerships.

To align philosophy and vision, answer:

- How well does our community understand our schools?
- How well do children understand the relevance of the material presented to them in school?
- What do children need to understand about their community?
- What does the community need to understand about schools?
- What experiences help children solidify information and push their thinking to higher levels?

- What resources are available within the community, and how do they relate to the Common Core State Standards?
- What is the importance of standards and benchmarks in learning, and how should students take ownership of them?

After answering these and other critical questions about beliefs, develop a "dashboard." A dashboard is a visual representation of the measures for success in any program, organization, or initiative. This dashboard will remind teachers of the clear direction and facilitate communication of the vision to stakeholders. The dashboard helps when naysayers attack or an implementation dip occurs.

A quick Internet search will elicit hundreds of examples of dashboards. The U.S. Education Dashboard (found at dashboard .ed.gov) and the dashboard for Birmingham Public Schools in Beverly Hills, Michigan (found at data-dashboard.birmingham .k12.mi.us) are both excellent examples.

Dashboard items can include:

- Partnership support
- Educational achievement
- Program sustainability
- Student and community engagement

Each category includes assessments to provide evidence documenting progress toward established goals. Evidence may include:

- Number of overall partnerships
- Number of curricular partnerships
- Student attendance
- Enrollment
- Student engagement surveys
- Partnership feedback
- Grades
- Benchmark attainment
- Changes in postsecondary enrollment data
- Passed referenda or propositions
- Monetary donations

Visual representations like these can be powerful. When something is visually displayed, it is a constant reminder of its importance and priority. Carefully select criteria of the greatest importance in your school or organization. Begin with those that match with the district mission. For instance, if student engagement and retention are important, select engagement surveys, attendance, and enrollment as the most important measures. Additional criteria can be added over time. One caution: Be careful not to create a data empire that dies of its own weight. Measure fewer items, but measure them well.

Create a Common Vocabulary

Once the philosophy is set, a dashboard can help show evidence of success by defining the new operation and explaining the technical aspects of it. The remaining steps do not need to be followed in any specific order, but they all need to be completed in order to prepare for a successful CBL experience.

Determine Roles and Responsibilities

CBL teachers still teach; however, to create a successful experience, they need to decide:

- Who will generate and map partnership possibilities and actual partners?
- Who will ensure curricular fidelity?
- Who will find and use software to track progress?
- Who is responsible for thanking partners?
- Who will be the liaison to the partners, the district office, or the Board of Education?
- Who will generate assessments geared toward the Common Core standards?
- Who will seek out necessary resources?

A classroom teacher starting a single experience may be able to address many of these issues alone, but a larger-scale implementation may require more strategizing. Innovation pushes boundaries. Understanding who has the power (whether implied or actual) to break through barriers to success is essential for the project's future. If roles and responsibilities are not formally assigned, identify key players so that when decisions need to be made, the path is clear.

Set Learning Goals

Marzano defined a learning goal as "a statement of what students will know and be able to do" (2007, p. 17). The definition of a "learning goal" does not change with CBL. Effective lessons begin with a clear statement of the learning goal (Hattie, 2009). In CBL, a new phrase—the unintentional benchmark—has been created. The unintentional benchmark is a benchmark that was attained but not stated as an intentional learning goal. The unintentional benchmark is realized through the teacher's or student's purposeful reflection but may have been attained even without realization.

Consider the story of Eileen, a fourth-grade teacher who was teaching a math lesson on money. Eileen's stated learning goal was to have students correctly make change. As she taught, students asked questions about the origins of the dollar. Eileen took time to guide the class through researching how the American dollar came to exist—obviously more of a social studies lesson. After the unit was done, Eileen reflected on the math benchmarks the students attained. She was not considering the social studies benchmarks that also were taught unintentionally. Later in the year, when Eileen reflected on a social studies unit she taught, it occurred to her that she had already met some of the benchmarks during the math discussion. She didn't set out to teach it, but the students learned anyway.

This is an unintentional benchmark. When teachers design a CBL lesson, they address a complex, integrated problem. Anticipating all of the benchmarks is nearly impossible. Reflection is key after the lesson has occurred to understand what students learned in the experience.

Often, teachers spend a great deal of time planning and carrying out a lesson. The CBL educator needs to spend a great deal of time on reflection as well. When formative assessment became regular practice, educators began spending more time analyzing the tests and changing practice based on the results (Ainsworth & Viegut, 2006). A true CBL experience is not complete until purposeful reflection takes place so that the student and the teacher understand the level of attainment for the stated benchmarks and the level of attainment of other curricular aspects that occurred as a result of the experience. The unintentional benchmark is not exclusive to the CBL experience. Every child makes connections differently, and most customized learning approaches allow for these connections to be recognized. Without purposeful reflection, educators lack a complete understanding of all that students were able to glean from the experience.

A second area requiring attention in relation to the learning goal is shared accountability. CBL requires increased understanding of how two entities share in the partnership's success. Shared accountability increases the relevance of the outcomes for the educator and the community partner.

For the community partner, the word "benchmark" might be totally foreign. Brillion High School in Brillion, Wisconsin, faced this challenge when educators developed their Ariens Technology and Engineering Education Center. The center is a collaborative effort between the school district and a local business partner, the Ariens Corporation (Nistler, Ariens Technology and Engineering Education Center | Blueprint: Designing Wisconsin's Future, 2009). Paul Nistler, principal of the high school, had to consider the use of the word "benchmark." The idea of trying to incorporate educational jargon into this community partnership did not seem like it would work, so the district uses the word "goal" instead. These goals are collaboratively developed between Ariens and the district so that students acquire the soft skills and core content necessary to for problem solving and adaptability. The district did not change the curriculum, just the words used to describe it, so that the community partner could be a true collaborator in the process.

Plan the Experience

Planning involves logistics. Consider these steps:

Find an Entry Point

Who is willing and able to take on the work? Perhaps a teacher wants to try a new instructional strategy or is struggling to reach students. Perhaps a partnership exists that could be scaled up to the next level. Maybe a well-defined curricular area could be made more relevant with a community partnership. Begin with a logical entry point. If one doesn't exist, consider making a cold call.

Make a Cold Call

For people to get on board with CBL, they need to understand its benefits to them. Convincing them requires helping them understand how a potential partnership improves the practice of the partner, the educator, and the students. Why would anyone attempt something new without seeing a personal or professional benefit? An educator seeking to develop a partnership needs to get comfortable about approaching a community partner with a completely unfamiliar idea, and then "selling" the partner on the experience. This is what those in the sales field call "making a cold call" (Connick, 2013).

A Boys and Girls Club's annual goal was raising awareness of the before- and afterschool opportunities the organization offered students. Jen, a Chicago-area educator, knew the organization's goal and also knew she needed help making afterschool tutoring more relevant to classroom outcomes. Jen set up a meeting with the club's director. The two of them arranged a partnership in which the teacher and the afterschool tutoring director had regular contact in order to ensure that tutoring would connect to classroom outcomes. The director of the Boys and Girls Club saw the collaboration as an opportunity to make students aware of the organization. The partnership gave the organization needed exposure, and it helped Jen raise student achievement. Without Jen making a cold call, the partnership—and positive outcomes—never would have happened.

Target Decision Makers

A business partner wanted to donate manufacturing equipment to a school in order to create a training facility and allow students to learn the manufacturing trade in class. The district thought it was on its way to a CBL relationship. As the superintendent prepared the final resolution for the Board of Education's approval, the partner discovered that board meetings were televised and withdrew the offer. This individual had not asked his supervisor for permission to do the project. He hoped to get the project started, and show his boss how well it was working, and then get the company's support.

The lesson in this experience is clear: Be sure the decision makers are in the room. If it is not possible to have the decision makers there, get their endorsement in writing. Identifying the people who actually can be a part of the learning experience, who can dedicate the necessary time and resources and walk hand-in-hand with educators, gets the job done.

Identify the Project's Curricular Goals

Educators and partners must decide together what the students will do. What will you teach? How will you teach it? How will it align with scope and sequence?

Educators may enter a partnership by pitching an idea, or the partner may have an activity that teachers align with their benchmarks. For example, imagine a school is working with a car dealership. The car dealer has sales data reflecting buying trends throughout the year and is wondering whether to adjust the number of sales people based on sales trends. The dealer presents the problem and asks for students to review the data and make a recommendation. Teachers likely would target the benchmark "analyze patterns and relationships" and have students study the situation. Or, had the car dealer offered to partner and the teachers said they were working on patterns and relationships, the dealer could have identified the trend analysis task as an activity that would fit with the school's benchmark. Either way, the partnership aligned with curricular needs.

CONNECTING STANDARDS WITHIN COMMUNITY PARTNERSHIPS

In Bozeman, Montana, students in the Bozeman Youth Initiative work with local coffee houses to compost coffee grounds. Volunteers in the Coffee 2 Compost (C2C) program range from middle schoolers to college students. The program has an identified learning goal for students, *"To encourage waste reduction and sustainability in communities"* (U.S. Environmental Protection Agency, 2011, p. 12). While the program does not explicitly teach science or environmental benchmarks, the C2C handbook is filled with scientific information students need to understand when they are working with partners (Baughman, 2011).

In another example, the Massachusetts Department of Education collaborated with the Massachusetts Service Alliance and Learn and Serve America on the publication *Community Lessons: Promising Curriculum Practices* (Bartsch et al., 2001). This publication is a collection of 14 curricular units for elementary to high schools organized in an eight-part framework.

(Continued)

Each of the units in the publication contains the same eight components, two of which are "rationale for connecting academic content" and "ways to assess academic and community outcomes" (Bartsch et al., 2001, p. vi). Teachers Michael Murray and Susan Waltuck of Sharon, Massachusetts, designed a unit for fifth graders through ninth graders that included 17 English language arts curricular strands that students would meet by identifying "everyday heroes" in their community (Bartsch et al., 2001, p. 46). Students are to identify and interview "ordinary citizens who have made extraordinary contributions to the Sharon community" (Bartsch et al., p. 47). Students develop the interview protocol and practice their interviewing, writing, listening, and speaking skills in addition to meeting content standards throughout the yearlong project.

CBL Link: CBL has teachers use an integrated curriculum approach to identify intentional benchmarks (learning goals) for students aligned to standards. The multidisciplinary approach causes educators to help students reach for higher benchmarks as they make the curriculum meaningful through a real-world setting. Teachers and students reflect to identify expected and unexpected benchmarks students have reached.

Design the Student and Program Assessments

In this new world of student learning objectives and the continued world of high-stakes accountability, educators' challenge is to set a floor for achievement and not a ceiling. Plan what evidence you will use to demonstrate success. You may show success by answering, "How is the curriculum more relevant for students?" and "What do students now know, and what are they able to now do?" (Marzano, 2003). Assessments might take the form of a survey or a paper-and-pencil test. More often, a CBL assessment has a nontraditional format. The experience has learning goals and targets, and they are measured through performance tasks, reflective journals, and benchmark tracking. High-quality CBL uses targets that are rigorous to challenge students, relevant so students are engaged, and assessments that cause students to take responsibility for achieving higher level learning. Assessments such as SMARTER Balanced, which are being written to align with the higher-order skills described in the Common Core, ask students to perform in this manner. Strategies such as CBL give students the opportunity to practice skills each day. Assessments crystallize student learning.

Planning for CBL requires time and reflection, but effective leaders know that spending time up front allows a good idea to be implemented well. The key to the implementation plan is finding the answers that work best for your context. That is the heart of customization and the CBL experience.

FRANKLIN SPRINGS INTO ACTION

Franklin Elementary School implemented a CBL experience following the five-part process. The principal, Jami, systematically worked to find the entry point, make the cold call, get to the decision makers, identify curricular goals, and design student and program assessments.

Find the entry point: District leaders discussing large-scale implementation of CBL wondered where it might take hold in a small way. Jami, Franklin Elementary's principal, was eager to embrace the district goal but was unsure how to make that happen. The superintendent heard about Jami's interest and approached her to ask her to create a significant CBL experience with an existing partner. Here were two entry points. The superintendent saw an opportunity with Jami's eagerness to be involved and made the call. Then Jami found the right connection in her community partnership to get the ball rolling. Educators should consider the person with whom they first want to communicate about the idea. Where is the best chance for success?

Make the cold call: This example includes two cold calls, the superintendent's call to Jami and Jami's call to her community partner. The superintendent met Jami at a local coffee shop to pitch the idea. After brainstorming possibilities together, Jami decided to approach the human resources manager at a local manufacturing firm she had already established a relationship with as a "Partner at Learning" (PAL). Jami's relationship with the company consisted of superficial, "feel-good" activities that had little to do with curriculum. Jami imagined a project that went far beyond the expectation for a PAL. She made sure to pitch the idea in a manageable way. She asked Sue, the human resources manager, if her team would like to talk about teaching part of the curriculum. Sue agreed, and a few weeks later, eight company managers sat down with Franklin's fifth-grade team to plan the project.

Get to the decision makers: Jami made sure that when she called the company, she contacted those who could decide whether to be involved. She connected with the human resources manager, who then collaborated with the department's vice president. These high-level executives were able to give the company's employees the necessary flexibility to meet with teachers and ultimately teach the unit lessons. If you begin with those who cannot make decisions on resources you will need, the entire venture is in jeopardy.

(Continued)

Identify curricular goals: Once Jami sat down with the company executives to discuss what the school wanted to do, they realized the objectives were fuzzy. As much as everyone wanted to do something great for kids, they had to figure out how business could intersect education. When the conversation in the room stalled, one educator returned to her lesson planning roots and raised the idea of learning activities. The company managers were full of ideas they wanted to try. When the educators analyzed those ideas through a learning lens, benchmarks began to appear. At the end of the first meeting, the managers said they would return with eight learning activities that mimicked the process of bringing an item from inception through sales. In a meeting a week later, the educators attached math, language arts, art, communication, problem solving, and soft skill benchmarks to each activity. What began as an unfocused brainstorming session crystallized into an eight-week curricular unit.

Design the program assessments: Measuring success is critical (Kennerly & Neely, 2003). People watched the program closely to check what students were learning. The company wanted to make sure it was worth employees' time, and district administrators wanted to ensure that CBL built goodwill between the community and school. The district needed to see that the students learned what they needed to learn, that the teachers were able to track curricular benchmarks to check for learning, and the community partner was treated in a way that resulted in a positive experience. Teachers created benchmark assessments to ensure students were learning. Administrators interviewed selected company managers to ensure they were satisfied and highlighted the endeavor in the community to show stakeholders the collaborative effort's success. There is power in shared outcomes. In the end, due to the experience's success, the business pledged its commitment to sustaining the partnership with Franklin in future years. Shared ownership made a difference.

Plan for Sustainability

Jacob started his principalship in a school without an established writing program or methodology. When he examined test scores and listened to stakeholder feedback, he realized writing was a critical need that had to be addressed. For four years, Jacob researched, planned, and led professional development to build systems within his school to support high-quality student writing. When he left his position for a new job, he worried about what would happen to student writing. The new principal did not see the need to give this area much attention. Jacob watched from afar, speaking to former colleagues and employees. Even without leadership, the student writing thrived. The systems Jacob had built and the capacity he helped others find survived his tenure.

When the leader who has championed work moves to a new position, the work has to sustain itself beyond that individual's time in the organization. CBL can be a leader's legacy if the leader sets a vision, plants the idea, helps it take root in appropriate places, supports it with appropriate resources, and then is open to new opportunities. CBL can persist after its champions are gone if it reaches a certain stage. Reaching that point requires planning.

Multiply Passion

Everyone likes to be on a winning team. When an effort is successful, it is important to capitalize on its success. CBL occurs incrementally, and advocates can build excitement by celebrating each step.

As we'll see later in Chapter 4, one urban high school was planning a pilot CBL program, and planners had to decide how many students the program could support. With three teachers and one CBL coach, they believed 75 was a reasonable number. They went to area middle schools to recruit students for the following year, but three days before the enrollment deadline, they had only 25 students. Downcast, they began to strategize alternatives even as others questioned the program. The teachers spoke to influential students they felt would learn well using the CBL approach and encouraged the students to take part. More students signed up and told their friends. In just three days, the program had more than 110 applicants, and the organizers had to use a lottery to select students. Suddenly those quiet critics were clamoring to be a part of the experience.

Each time that CBL is successful, more people will want to be involved. Find a way to include them. Teachers outside the CBL experience could offer curricular expertise. Students not enrolled could give their opinions on final products or presentations. Community members who see a successful CBL experience could take part in the next experience. Wherever there is interest, there is potential to build on it in future. Capitalize on that interest.

Create a Three-Month Legacy

Janet Jackson's song "What Have You Done for Me Lately?" expresses a sentiment at the core of the sustainability plan. Once CBL has had some successes, it is easy to rest on that success. A legacy isn't something to be assessed when you are leaving a position. It must be regularly tended. To sustain CBL, have a meaningful opportunity every three months.

Keeping change at the forefront keeps the experience active and makes it a part of the culture, especially before it becomes systematized (Lewin, 1947). What can one person do to sustain CBL? A potential cycle involves strategizing.

> ***By the end of October:*** Cultivate a new community partnership to build a relationship.

> ***By the end of January:*** Implement a partnership and assess its effectiveness to elevate the relationship. Fuse formative assessment data from multiple perspectives to continuously improve upon the process.

> ***By the end of May:*** Celebrate the partnership's success, presenting it publicly and recognizing those involved. Let the partner know how much their contribution is appreciated in order to deepen the relationship and future possibilities.

The cycle may seem simple, but imagine every educator in a district following it.

Someone more experienced in project-based instructional practices or community relations might follow a different cycle. For a teacher with some project-based experience, the cycle may look like this:

> ***By the end of October:*** Design one project-based lesson with a CBL level community partner (See the Partnership Pyramid, Figure 1.1). A single lesson can be a manageable and valuable learning experience for students and teachers.

> ***By the end of January:*** Design a comprehensive, project-based *unit* with a CBL level community partner. Once educators and students have mastered the CBL instructional approach using a single lesson, they are better able to expand their practice in a whole unit.

By the end of May: Design a student performance assessment that allows students to demonstrate 21st century and soft skills they gained through the year's CBL experiences. The type of assessment should match the learning outcome (Webb, 2002). Many educators will need to cultivate the skills to create effective assessments, research effective project-based assessments, and align the practice to the outcomes of the CBL experience. Once mastered, CBL assessment is a powerful tool in the teacher's toolbox.

These cycles have the potential to have a significant effect on the community, student engagement, and student learning. Once teachers are skilled at creating CBL experiences, they may be able to expedite the process and move the cycle to monthly increments rather than quarterly.

Develop a Communication Plan

Getting the word out is important to any change initiative. Leaders who want to implement CBL have to take every opportunity to point out how it can address current issues.

A Board of Education subcommittee was lamenting the lack of relevant educational experiences for students. One committee member said, "I am so *frustrated!* Why are we asking our kids to engage in drill and kill? How can we get them excited about school?" A district administrator and CBL proponent pointed out the effect CBL was having in the district. The conversation lasted less than five minutes but had a strong impact.

The "elevator speech," a summary of key points that you could deliver during the time it takes to ride the elevator, is a powerful technique that can change an organization's future. Small chats happen everywhere. Mastering the elevator speech requires practice and understanding your core values. The elevator speech helps leaders connect their agenda to what is relevant and important to the person they are trying to persuade.

In cases where CBL already is succeeding, scaling up is still possible. Nominate partners for awards. Highlight projects at a school board meeting. Invited media to report on partnerships and performance assessments. Intentionally communicating each step of planning a CBL experience impacts its success.

POSSIBILITIES FOR SCALING UP

The *New York Times* partners with the Bank Street College of Education in New York City to collaboratively develop lesson plans connecting the curriculum to real-life situations. These units are called *The Daily Lesson Plan*. For example, the plan for April 22, 2009, was titled "An Arm and a Leg: Measuring the Impact of the Recession on Families and Communities." The lesson helped students understand how the loss of health care coverage and other factors from the recession affected the economy and families (Sandhya, 2009). Students researched by interviewing community members for their perspectives.

Scaling Up: A teacher using this lesson plan could involve a local health care provider or local insurance agents to help students understand multiple facets of the issue.

The INSPIRE project, conducted by researcher Katie Carlisle (2011) of Georgia State University, used an existing partnership to create a new opportunity. The local school and a neighboring university worked together to use the performing arts curriculum to teach lessons during Black History Month. Graduate students in the music education program collaborated with teachers at the school on the curriculum for a group of middle school students. After the experience, the students were able to articulate how to use a performing art to tell a story from Black history.

Scaling Up: This project was a research study but has potential for a long-term partnership. A core component of CBL is the collaborative planning that was demonstrated in this study. Sustaining the project's success beyond the study could build CBL and a strong relationship between school and community.

Map the Partnerships to Know the Playing Field

Mapping out partnerships is another way to build a foundation for CBL. Use the partnership pyramid in Chapter 1 to determine and catalogue the partnership level of your effort. Mapping is important because as partnerships grow and expand, managing them can become daunting. By identifying what the partnerships look like and how the partner's assets are being used, a district minimizes the possibility of overextending the partner relationship—asking the same organization to partner multiple times can wear out the relationship. Tracking resources helps reserve and use available resources in the most appropriate way. The partnership pyramid from Chapter 1 is especially handy in defining the partnerships and the level of involvement for each. Who are the partners? Who are they working with? What are they doing in the district? Visual representations allow educators to see whether a partnership already exists and where an effort can be scaled up.

Another mapping tool is a sociogram, a concept developed by Jacob Moreno (1953). A sociogram visually represents how community stakeholders interact. Figure 3.2 (Sample Sociogram) is a simplified version of a sociogram. The tool allows a person to map existing partnerships. Here, the district has also listed the level of partnership based on the partnership pyramid. Using the sociogram, those wishing to engage in CBL can see where opportunities exist. For example, Partner A is labeled "partnership." Potential exists to scale up to a full CBL experience.

Partnerships can be tracked simply using a spreadsheet. Educators can track active partners and communicate with stakeholders. Table 3.1, Partnership Tracking Spreadsheet, is a tool educators can use to assist them in understanding their current relationships.

Figure 3.2   Sample Sociogram

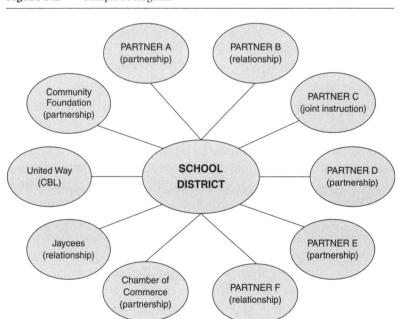

The information in a tracking tool can be sorted to identify areas of strength and opportunities to scale up. Educators in this district can see, for example, that ACME Corp. has been asked to dedicate resources more than once, but another organization may not have been asked at all.

Mapping out partners allows educators to see where possibilities exist for improvement; it allows them to scale up. Again, looking at Table 3.1, one can see that Langston Phillips is involved as a partner and not with curriculum. Might Langston be willing to become involved on a deeper level? It is certainly worth a conversation to find out.

Embed School Improvement

High-quality school improvement plans cause educators to change their practice. CBL can be written into an improvement goal as a SMART (strategic and specific, measurable, attainable, result-oriented, time bound) goal. For example, to increase CBL's presence, a logical goal might be: By the end of the school year, four teachers will have developed a new CBL unit around five or more Common Core standards. A teacher might connect this goal to a student achievement goal: by the end of the semester, 85% of students will achieve a 3 or 4 (proficient or distinguished) on the CBL performance rubric.

Don't stop with incorporating CBL into the school improvement plan. Create a dashboard showing what you want to see, and then regularly revisit it to assess progress with your staff

Table 3.1   Partnership Tracking Spreadsheet

Name of Partner Organization	Contact Person	Level of Partnership	Name of School Contact	Description of Activity	Dates
ACME Corp.	Elizabeth Parks	Joint Curriculum	Marshall Jackson	Self-Advocacy Class	Fall 2013
Smith Car Dealership	Langston Phillips	Partnership	Grade 3 @ Lakeside School	Community PALS Program	2013–14 school year
ACME Corp.	Steven Smith	CBL	Marshall Jackson	Stock Portfolio Management	Spring 2013

(Strand, 2008). David Mann (2010) in his book *Creating a Lean Culture: Tools to Sustain Lean Conversations* states, "The status of virtually every project should be visual" (p. 53). He goes on to say that "visuals give the leader the ability to . . . move to action" (p. 24). A constant progress reminder is good practice for any project to help keep people accountable.

Implement the Initiative

One veteran superintendent frequently reminds his staff, "We don't *plan* to implement. We implement." He isn't advocating a "ready, fire, aim" approach. He is suggesting not being afraid to get started, even if the implementation plan isn't perfect.

Some factors to consider when implementing CBL:

Don't Be Tempted by Mediocrity

A good idea poorly implemented is a bad idea (Guskey, 2002). In the previous example from Franklin Elementary, one staff member suggested forgetting about planning and vision and just getting as many partnerships off the ground as possible. The superintendent knew his teachers and administrators were not all as ready and willing as Jami, so he gently downplayed the suggestion that a mass partnership drive be created. Educators cannot afford to implement CBL haphazardly or they risk alienating partners.

A learning director who did not believe in CBL was told by her superintendent that she needed to foster CBL in the district. Wanting to follow directions, she quickly developed a high school class with the local newspaper. The relationship between the district and the newspaper was already tenuous. Then the learning director decided to let the newspaper pitch the class to the students with little oversight from her. When the day came, the newspaper editor gave a three-hour "sit and get" presentation to the high school students. Only a handful of students registered for the class, and the class was cancelled. This experience hurt an already shaky relationship between the newspaper and the district. Just because CBL *can* be done does not mean that it should be done without buy-in and understanding of the concept.

Do Not Underestimate the Importance of Reflection

Schedule time to talk to all of the parties involved throughout the process. Formatively assess their level of engagement, learning, and needs. Adjust the plan as necessary throughout implementation, and even revise it afterward to improve the next cycle. Regularly collect and analyze data in order to continuously improve.

Beware of Negative Partners

Some partnerships sour. Adjustment may mean scaling back if the situation warrants. Be respectful but firm to preserve the relationship so that student learning is not harmed. For example, a businessman running for school board approached the business classes at a high school about teaching students. He wanted to explain appropriate business planning. This was also his platform in a bid for a seat on the school board. The businessman insisted that the district's $35 million in referendum-approved building debt was cause for the district to stop spending and increase class sizes. Politically, the partnership was disadvantageous and potentially inappropriate, but district administrators wanted to be respectful to this man. The superintendent intervened and suggested that the man's financial agenda remain in open session at the board room until the election was over. After the election, the man no longer wanted to teach, and he quietly removed himself from all district involvement.

Celebrate What Works

Sometimes the partnership doesn't achieve what you thought it might. Recognize what succeeded, and plan to be better the next time. Teachers and partners need encouragement just as students do. When something doesn't work quite as planned, embrace that fact and move forward.

Assess and Improve

In many cases, CBL starts small. Systematizing the concept is crucial for its long-term success. CBL has the potential to interrelate within the existing structures so that it can take hold. CBL asks educators to change instructional delivery, not content. Instead of changing to a new system, CBL changes how the system operates. Peter Senge says a "shift of mind" (Senge, 2011, p. 4) is required from stakeholders when working toward systemization. For CBL to succeed, it needs to be on everyone's radar. Then administrators can meet individuals where they are and help them grow in the practice. Senge (2011) encourages seeing "patterns rather than static snapshots." This happens in several ways.

Think PreK–18

PreK–18 councils work to develop systemic thinking in education and help educators in institutions from prekindergarten through postsecondary collaborate to ensure students' seamless progression. The goal is to develop fully functioning members of society. Wiggins and McTighe (1998) refer to "backward design." When teachers begin with the end in mind, they are better able to see what students should know and be able to do, and then plan accordingly to ensure students achieve those outcomes. CBL links education to the skills students need in order to succeed in their posteducation lives. If institutions of higher education expect students to be able to apply their learning to future careers, then creating partnerships and adjusting curricular delivery to apply learning throughout a student's educational career is a logical goal for K–12 educators.

Leverage Assessments

As Peter Drucker said, "What gets measured gets managed." To achieve CBL, evaluate employees on whether they are using high-quality CBL. To see students use higher-order thinking skills, assess those skills. To have experts share their knowledge in schools, create a dashboard to track the number of partners involved. Include the goal in the school improvement plan, ask employees to make it their personal goal, and make it your personal goal. Systemic measurement changes practice and ultimately achieves results (Senge, 1990). Tables 3.2 (Educator Rubric), 3.3 (Community Rubric), and 3.4 (Student Rubric) are examples of possible CBL assessment rubrics. The student rubric

Table 3.2   Educator Rubric

	Exploring	Emerging	Achieving	Exceeding
	The community partner has shown interest in working with the school.	The community partner has shown interest in CBL and has worked with the school on 1 or 2 lessons.	The community partner has successfully completed a CBL experience by engaging in cooperative planning and instruction with an educator.	The community partner has successfully completed a CBL experience and has made a long-term commitment to the strategy with the school.
	The community partner has a professional relationship with an educator.	The community partner's experience was positive, but there were limited shared outcomes.	The community partner's experience was positive and achieved its expected outcomes.	The community partner's experience was positive and exceeded expected outcomes.
COMMUNITY	The community partner has a positive attitude toward working with the school.	The community partner increased its awareness of the school/district.	The community partner knows more about the school/district and education in general and speaks positively of the district in its regular interactions with others.	As a result of its involvement, the community partner becomes a vocal advocate for the school/district.

Table 3.3 Community Rubric

	Exploring	Emerging	Achieving	Exceeding
EDUCATOR	The educator has a positive, professional relationship with a potential partner.	The educator has shown interest in CBL and worked with a partner on 1 or 2 lessons.	The educator has successfully completed a CBL experience by engaging in cooperative planning and instruction with a community partner.	The educator has fully committed to a foundational framework of CBL instruction.
	The educator has explored current units and/or lessons for CBL potential.	The educator has identified relevant benchmarks that should be attained in the CBL lessons.	Through the CBL experience, the educator facilitated student achievement of multiple curricular benchmarks.	The teacher has mastered the ability to track benchmarks and facilitates CBL experiences that allow students to achieve multiple intentional and unintentional benchmarks.
	The educator has a desire to educate innovatively.	The educator has identified (and possibly communicated with) potential partners that align with curricular lessons or units.	The educator has an increased understanding of the relevance of the curricular material to the community setting.	The educator has strong curricular connections to the entire community.
		The educator reflects and offers opinions on the CBL experience.	The educator intentionally seeks feedback and adjusts CBL based on that feedback.	The educator practices regular reflection and refinement on CBL skills and experiences.

Table 3.4   Student Rubric

	Exploring	Emerging	Achieving	Exceeding
STUDENT	The student understands he is part of a larger community. The student has knowledge of community organizations. The student has a desire to learn in a way that is different from traditional educational offerings.	The student takes part in the CBL experience and understands the learning goals. The student is exposed to a community partner and knows that partner's profession. The student's experience was positive.	The student has achieved curricular benchmarks through a CBL experience. The student has a better understanding of a specific community partner and that partner's role in society. The student's experience was positive and kept her engaged and active throughout the learning process.	Student retention of information presented in the CBL experience exceeds that of a traditional classroom. The student is inspired to become more deeply involved with this or another community organization as a result of the CBL experience. The student's experience caused her to seek out related information beyond the curricular expectations.

45

focuses on student retention, awareness of community, and engagement. These may be appropriate measures for your setting, or they may need to be tailored to suit your particular outcomes. The same is true for the educator and community rubrics. Here, the focus for the educator is on curriculum, assessment, instruction (using CBL), and community connections. Community partners are assessed on their participation, engagement, and advocacy. The essence of the rubrics is critical—measuring outcomes increases the likelihood of success. The specifics are up to you.

Classroom assessments matter, too. Measuring 21st century skills is challenging. The assessments look different. More large-scale tests are being created to align with the Common Core and potentially measure higher-order thinking skills, but until educators are certain these tests measure what is important, they need their own measures. Classroom assessments can rarely be paper-and-pencil tests. The true CBL experience allows for individualized learning, which means students will be ready to demonstrate their skills and abilities at different times during the year. Teachers' first priority cannot be common summative moments, although they do need to check to make sure students are on track. First, teachers must concentrate on being guides on the side to help students see where their learning journey is headed and where they need to go next.

Teachers in a large high school in a high-poverty area were teaching a unit of CBL lessons on "Why Countries Go to War." Initially, students selected the war they wanted to study with the caveat that their choice had to be recent enough that they could interview living veterans for their final project. Students met social studies benchmarks by researching the wars' backgrounds. For science, they studied the use of chemical warfare in the war and the agents' effects on the human body. They met English benchmarks by interviewing veterans and writing final reports. Students worked with local reporters to learn interviewing skills. They also worked with local taxi and bus companies to arrange transportation to visit local veterans. The students either brought veterans to the school or visited them personally to listen to firsthand accounts of the wars. Students used excerpts from the interviews in videos that were debuted at the grand opening of a community War Museum that they and veterans attended.

Rather than a multiple-choice test on war, the video was used as a more meaningful assessment of the students' understanding. The teachers were analyzing to see if students had synthesized information about the wars to form appropriately deep and thoughtful questions for the veterans. Educators also assessed students' communication and problem-solving skills as the students conducted the interviews: When a veteran took the conversation in an unexpected direction, did the student have enough mastery of the content to redirect, incorporate, or assimilate that information into the conversation? After the projects were completed, the teachers assessed how the students edited the pieces to honestly reflect the conversation yet stay within the time limits while addressing the unit's core concepts. The teachers knew these were the outcomes, and the CBL experience was designed around them. The way they assessed student learning drove their instructional practice. By beginning with a high-level assessment, teaching practices rise to higher levels.

Planning a CBL experience will take some time, but once educators are skilled at the practice, the time commitment will be reduced. This framework offers educators one way to examine the practice of CBL and reflect on the important steps necessary to ensure success.

Questions for Reflection

1. Right now in our school/district, how is content connected to real-world application?
2. What do students know of the expertise in our community?
3. Are students aware of how the members of community organizations/businesses apply skills in our curriculum?

CHAPTER 4

Case Study: Community– Based Learning School

MAIN IDEA

Studying an example of how a group of educators* successfully developed community-based learning within a high school despite real challenges can help educators see ways to implement a similar initiative.

THE BEGINNING OF COMMUNITY–BASED LEARNING SCHOOL

Unified School District was struggling with its relationship with the community. Like many districts across the United States, Unified had financial difficulties. Unstable finances caused significant administrative and teacher turnover. With many educators not having been in their jobs for long, the district struggled to create and sustain community partners in the city of approximately 62,000. With a new core of administrators, novice educators, and a disconnected community, the culture was less than positive. Some educators might distance themselves in such a culture by retreating into the solitude of their own classroom and closing the door on new opportunities with the changes. Others see the possibility for innovative thinking. Four educators at South High School were such innovators.

In late winter 2012, James (a peer coach and instructional support teacher), Beth (an English teacher), and Ron (a social studies teacher) went to their high school principal, Steven, with an issue. These seasoned educators wanted to do something about the boredom they saw regularly in their students. Each had independently researched project-based learning (PBL) and was ready to try something different. They went to the principal with the idea of combining social studies and English into a cross-curricular, PBL class.

With the principal's support, the teachers approached a district office employee. Kelly was known for supporting well-developed innovative practices. She not only embraced their idea, she expanded on it.

The district wanted to strengthen community partnerships. Kelly had been researching community-based learning (CBL) and the high school teachers' proposal seemed like an opportunity to explore the idea. James, Beth, and Ron had considered combining only two subject areas because of logistics. Kelly asked them to set aside logistical concerns and think about what they really wanted to do.

Ultimately, they decided, they would like to combine the core areas into a four-hour block of time and teach English, math, social studies, and science as a cohesive PBL experience. Kelly worked with them to eliminate each obstacle—class size, not enough time, no other teachers, the complexity of high school math. In the financial squeeze, the district had adopted a minimum class size of 28 students per section as a cost-saving measure. Kelly and the teachers petitioned the board of education for a waiver to form more manageable classes of 25 students.

The team tentatively planned to start in fall 2012, with the option to postpone if planning time ran short. Eleanor, a science teacher from the middle school who had a passion for PBL, joined the team after the teachers association worked through the displacement caused by Eleanor's presence. Incorporating math was the final hurdle. Instead of their dream of four hours and four content areas in a block of cross-curricular project-based instruction, the team settled on three hours and three content areas in a PBL block.

The teachers' original goal was student-centered: to change instruction from lecture to project-based. Once again, Kelly stretched their thinking. She asked, "How could the PBL block be structured to incorporate community partnerships?" She explained the concept of CBL, informing the team that the superintendent had asked her to research the practice and foster its implementation. At first, the teachers were skeptical. They didn't want to take on too much, and the leap to project-based learning seemed enough.

Kelly listened intently to their concerns then questioned them about their goals. What did they want students to be able to do? How would they keep students engaged? Kelly explained that the teachers had a golden opportunity to bring the community closer to the district. She helped them see that the more they related student learning to the real world, the more students would see the relevance of their classwork. James, Ron, Beth, and Eleanor wanted time to think about the idea.

Two weeks later, the team came to Kelly with a rough outline of eight study units encompassing English, social studies, and science benchmarks for ninth and tenth grades. Each unit was designed around a core community partnership. The team had decided to call itself Community-Based Learning School.

Steven, South High's principal, was nervous about creating a new school within the school. He wanted this opportunity to succeed but worried that a new school would cause students to not identity with South High School. Steven and the Community-Based Learning staff considered whether the school should be a charter, a magnet, a pilot, or something else completely. In the end, to keep student identity within the school, the team decided not to seek grant funding and to become an educational program. The school was renamed Community-Based Learning at South High School. Students who signed up for Community-Based Learning elected a three-credit class in which they would earn a science, social studies, and English grade.

Eleanor, Beth, and Ron would teach the three content areas, but James's place on the team was not secure. He was an instructional coach, not a core content instructor. He was one of the most passionate team members of the team, however, and the team needed his curricular expertise to keep the vision aligned. Kelly backed a proposal designating James as a CBL coordinator—a move that needed board of education approval. With projected budget tightening, the position was a tough sell. The first attempt resulted in a tabled discussion. James continued as part of the team without knowing if he would actually be able to take part.

MAKING PROGRESS

The timeline for CBL at South High School was set. It was now March, and the teachers needed students. They presented their idea at the middle schools, to current ninth graders, and to prospective parents. They were told they needed a minimum of 75 students to enact the program at South High School. As is often the case, students' social network came into play. Once a few students signed up, interest began to grow. The team ended up needing a lottery when more than 100 students applied.

With the demonstrated support, Kelly once again addressed the board of education about the position of CBL coordinator. The board remained reluctant to approve a new position while the district faced financial trouble, but Kelly, knowing that board members also valued innovative practices, pointed out that not only did the new program bring in students from outside the district thereby increasing district revenue, but it promoted the instructional practices the board had been exploring for the last year. After a grueling question-and-answer session, Kelly convinced the board that the investment would be worth the returns, and members approved the new position. James applied and was appointed CBL coordinator. The team was finally set.

With students enrolled, teachers in place, administration on board, and a skeletal curriculum, the team began the difficult work. Educators do not always have philosophical discussions when they plan a new initiative. In this case, the team made sure members discussed their beliefs, vision, and goals. The teachers visited schools around the state and country to find a framework around which to build CBL at South High School. In May 2012, four months after pitching the idea to administration, Kelly and the team traveled to San Francisco for the National Coalition for Community Schools Symposium. The conference provided the framework they were seeking.

The Coalition for Community Schools did not focus on CBL, but it did open team members' eyes to the idea of community learning centers (CLCs). The premise of CLCs is that community members work hand in hand with educators to wrap around services that meet students' full range of needs: mental health, wellness, tutoring, after and before school care, and so on. The idea caused the teachers to pause. What they learned at the symposium was amazing, but they did not feel able to build a CLC. Kelly reminded the team that that the first small step for them was academic. By focusing on CBL and incorporating community partners into the learning process, they build a support base to draw upon later as they reached the point of considering a CLC. The team created a long-range vision with the learning center in mind. Meanwhile, they focused on creating CBL experiences for the 2012–13 school year and began a summer schedule of planning.

CHALLENGES ARISE

As the school year ended, the team encountered two roadblocks. Eleanor, the science teacher, had asked to be moved from the middle school to join the high school team. She received the transfer, but at the same time, enrollment in science courses dropped. Because of the district's financial difficulties and the lower enrollment, the high school needed to reduce a portion of a science position.

Other staff blamed the CBL team and said Eleanor's position was displacing a science teacher. Steven designed a creative schedule so no one lost a job, but that did not appease the science team. Some believed that the CBL team thought their science offering would somehow be better than the general offerings.

Steven's solution was to offer a portion of the CBL science teaching load to any science teacher who would like it. Team members were worried. They knew that teachers in this endeavor had to believe in community schools and the CBL philosophy. They wondered how to integrate a new member so late in the process, but they accepted the principal's decision. Kyle, a veteran high school science teacher, joined the team.

The teachers' second barrier was accountability. How would this team measure success? The team's core goals focused on community engagement and student achievement. Board members and other teachers began to ask how the CBL school teachers would know whether the educational rigor was adequate. The board of education continued to have questions: How much would this initiative cost? What kind of resources would it generate? The team needed professional development and technology to support student engagement in self-directed learning. How successful would the instruction be? Would students be more engaged? Would the team sustain the opportunity beyond one year?

Kelly, Steven, and the team worked to create clear measures of success. They decided to track student achievement, partnership support, and student engagement. The team next needed to determine the definition of success for each measure, and they needed a high-quality instrument to measure it. They wanted to use the state standardized test to measure student achievement, but the exam occurred only once a year. For a day-to-day measure of student success, the team set benchmarks and created a spreadsheet to use to track student proficiency as students completed the curricular units. The team would measure the percentage of benchmarks each student attained to determine student achievement.

Partnership support was divided into two categories: financial and academic. The team developed a spreadsheet of partners and tracked their contributions. Some community partners gave in-kind donations of their products, others assisted with instruction in the classes, and some gave money to the team because they believed in the new school. For example, a local business gave the team its used furniture so that the school didn't have to purchase new tables. The team noted the contribution on the donation tracking form.

The remaining focus was how students felt about the experience. Kelly had researched engagement and student autonomy. She knew that having engaged students was critical to CBL's success. She also believed that students would be engaged if the team created a high-quality autonomous educational opportunity. The question was how to measure engagement. The team decided to measure retention within the program and survey students. The survey asked students their views on items like autonomy and interest. The team decided to give the survey at the beginning and end of the year to see whether the participating in CBL would change students' opinions in these areas.

The teachers discussed whether to include grants as a measure of success. They had already received a few small grants, yet were unsure how much time they would have to continue to write grants. They decided to leave out grants as a measure for the time being.

CREATING A CURRICULUM

Planning measures, securing staff, and enrolling students took the team until summer 2012. The teachers had three months to flesh out the curricular skeleton to be ready for students in September. As sometimes happens with innovations, however, team members got bogged down in logistics. Conversations that began about designing a unit diverged into technology require-ments, supplies, and room set up. Team members redirected themselves often. Just when they thought they all were moving in the same direction, the science teacher who joined the team last began to question the work. Kyle was not interested in meeting as frequently as the other team members were, and he often was not present to give his opinion when the team made decisions. When Kyle did return, he did not agree with the team's direction. In late July, despite the decision that had allowed him to join the team to keep a place in the school, Kyle opted to remove himself from the group. The principal had tried to create a situation so that the other science department teachers wouldn't blame the CBL school for the decrease in general science enrollment, a move that may have been smart politically but now had turned out to be detri-mental to the team. With Kyle's withdrawal, the CBL team had yet another adjustment to make.

Team members decided to stop planning the curriculum with only one unit fully designed—enough to get them through the first six weeks of school. Aptly, the unit was called "CBL." They had partnered with a researcher from a nearby university doing a neigh-borhood project in which he collected data from people about their perceptions of their neighborhoods. The researcher was having difficulty finding young subjects and gaining access to the home-bound. The team and the professor realized that students could explore their neighborhoods, speak to residents, and collect these data.

The team got district permission to assist in the study and aligned curricular benchmarks to the experience. Students would explore their neighborhoods through the lens of each subject area. First, they would identify plants and animals native to the area. Next, they would talk to their neighbors about why they lived there and what they liked about the neighborhood. Finally, students would photograph scenes that best represented their neighbor-hoods and develop a gallery presentation of what they had learned.

As the opening of school approached, the team was frazzled. Members had been working nonstop since December, and even with all of the time and energy they had invested, they felt unpre-pared. They continued to encourage one another and struggled to maintain their energy. One week before school started, the teach-ers took a chance and invited students and their families to a cook-out to kick off the school year. Ninth and tenth graders typically do not come to school with their parents and generally are reluc-tant to give up one of their last evenings of summer. However, nearly every enrollee attended, a large morale boost for the team and the students. The team was relying on every such small win to stay motivated. It was all they had until the first day of school.

As the year began, students were highly engaged and teach-ers were motivated. The media visited and wrote stories about the school, donations continued to come in, and partnership opportu-nities were abundant. It seemed everyone was excited to be part of a winning team.

SETBACK

The beginning of the school year went very well. Students were excited about the new opportunity and highly engaged in school. Parents and community members were very involved with the school and were talking all over the city about this new and exciting program. As they neared the end of their first six-week unit,^ the CBL team began work on their planned assessment. While planning the curriculum for the school, the team had decided to conclude each unit with students demonstrating their learning in a performance assessment. For the neighborhood unit, each student would use a photo from their neighborhood and prepare a presentation on why the photo best represented where they lived. The students then had a gallery walk where teachers, administrators, members of the community and board of education, and partners could hear the students present. Students answered questions about their projects and about the CBL school.

The student presentations were going well until one disgruntled science teacher arrived. The science teachers were still upset by the reduced position from lower enrollment, and this particular teacher seemed intent on looking for evidence of inferiority in the new school. The teacher stopped in front of one student, and instead of asking about the project, the school, or the partnership goals, asked, "Can you identify the tree in your picture?" The student could not. The teacher then proclaimed that CBL students didn't know science.

Team members learned two important things: that some people were waiting to attack the innovation to prove that traditional school was the only way to learn, and that they should publicly display the benchmarks students were working to attain. In this instance, students were expected to be able to use a taxonomic key to identify plants. This benchmark addressed mastery of a lifelong skill rather than rote memorization. The team learned its lesson and adjusted performance assessments.

EXCEEDING EXPECTATIONS

Despite the one negative response, the team found the project went far beyond members' expectations. The teachers had thought they were concluding a CBL unit, but after the gallery walk, the university professor invited the students to give their presentations in a neighborhood gallery walk at a local restaurant. The professor told colleagues, community business leaders, and his friends about the experience, and word began to spread throughout the community. The professor's supportive response, the additional presentation opportunity for students, and the community buzz were unanticipated outcomes of the community partnership. The CBL team believed in the concept, but the added outcomes strengthened their beliefs in the practice.

The team honed their skills in CBL, and partnerships increased. They planned a second unit on elections. Students created websites to inform voters about political issues of which to be aware. The co-founder of a national political news organization tailored a message and sent it to the students. Local politicians came to speak to classes about the governmental process. On Election Day, students engaged in a "get out the vote" campaign. As the unit progressed, the teaching team felt tugged toward traditional ways of teaching and occasionally reverted to presenting material and testing students on the material with a paper-and-pencil exam. After several months, though, they mastered true teaching for understanding.

In December, the team took students to a board of education meeting. Board members were beginning to discuss the budget discussions, and the team wanted to show that the class size waiver and coordinator's position were warranted. After students and teachers spoke about the CBL experience, several parents attested to the difference they saw in their children. Although the stories were individual and not collective data, students said they felt more engaged in school and learning, retained more content and skills, and demonstrated soft skills in their presentations. Board members were impressed and supported the innovative effort.

The team completed the year with excellent results. The teachers established more than 40 formal community partnerships and elicited more than $12,000 of in-kind and cash donations. Each curricular unit involved more partners to enhance students' learning. The end-of-year student survey showed more than 90% of students had high engagement scores, teacher-student relationships were more positive, and students' confidence in their communication and collaboration skills increased. Students became skilled at tracking benchmarks and directing their own learning, and they improved the number of benchmarks they attained. The student retention rate was more than 80%, and the school was expanded to include eleventh and twelfth grades. The team ended the year by winning a large grant to foster their vision of a CLC at the school.

Creating a CBL school at South High School led teachers to conclude

- Success breeds success. The positive reaction from community partners after they completed their partnership led others to want to be involved with the school and increased community support for the district overall.

- The team succeeded because teachers measured what was important. What is measured gets attention.
- Ongoing learning caused team members to continually refine their practices so that the experience was as engaging and authentic as possible for students.
- Despite the barriers to success, the team's dedication to its vision allowed members to persevere even in the face of adversity.
- This change effort, although significant, was small. In a high school of 1,300 students, CBL involved 75. The teachers interviewed those students and found that the year had made a significant difference in their attitudes toward learning and school. A majority of the students were more self-driven than when they began.
- Innovation requires resources. James's position was critical for success. The district's commitment even with limited resources was necessary for the school to succeed.

The CBL staff were self-motivated and dedicated. Their energy and passion got the work done. Community-Based Learning School at South High School was a significant undertaking. Less complex CBL projects are being implemented all over the country. CBL can be as large or as small as planners decide their school and community need.

*Names have been changed.
^See Appendix A for a sample unit plan from a school similar to Community-Based Learning School.

Questions for Reflection

1. What parts of this case study might be simple to implement in our setting? Which parts seem difficult? Why?
2. Community-Based Learning School faced down detractors as educators implemented the new programming. What detractors might we face in our setting?
3. Where would I have acted differently than the educators in this case study? Why? Where would I have acted similarly?
4. Community-Based Learning School was successful in large part due to the teachers spearheading the initiative. Who are the educators in our school/district who have this type of passion and leadership ability? How might they be inspired to start an endeavor like Community-Based Learning School?

CHAPTER 5

Essential Practices in Community–Based Learning

MAIN IDEA

Community-based learning is built around a flexible framework that allows educators to adopt innovative practices, adapting them as necessary to produce success.

Many educators have participated in labor-intensive change efforts such as curriculum mapping, implementing balanced literacy programs, technology initiatives, data retreats, and creating common formative assessments, all of which can have a significant impact on student achievement. Yet these initiatives require the collaboration and time of many coworkers.

In community-based learning (CBL), the individual educator can be a change agent and create CBL experiences within the existing structure. One person can inspire students to be engaged learners who take responsibility for their own learning.

In a relatively short period of time, one person can be flexible, adaptive, and responsive with new partners, and those individual actions can lead to revolutionary systemic change.

Once CBL gestates in a locale, it can grow quickly. Leaders who promote the experience, recognize participants for their high-quality work, and continuously communicate the concept get others excited about making a difference in children's education. Recall Jami's example from Chapter 3 (Franklin Springs Into Action, pp. 32–33). People in her district saw the CBL experience teachers were engaged in, and the next week she had three more teachers come to her with new CBL ideas.

Whether in charter, private, or public schools, only high-quality institutions will succeed in the future (National Commission on Teaching and America's Future, 2013). Critics of current practices in public education believe that educators' work should be measured. As educational accountability increases, policymakers are demanding an efficient way to collect data in order to label schools successful or unsuccessful.

The challenge for educators is to measure the right things. With the Common Core State Standards and the P21 Framework (Partnership for 21st Century Skills, 2011), policymakers have signaled a desire to shift from requiring students to acquire content to demanding that they master higher level thinking. Educators who hang on to what they have always known and done and fail to innovate will find themselves behind (Wagner, 2010). Leaders willing to create lasting systems of high quality through next-generation thinking will create thriving schools.

DRINKING THE GOOD WINE FIRST

When it comes to CBL or almost any endeavor, success will breed success. If you can "knock it out of the park" with the first experience, positive responses will help in creating the next experience. CBL involves developing relationships. A successful beginning is one in which partners *like* being a part of the experience. When CBL is done well, new relationships will be built among students, teachers, and community members.

To build the relationships that are CBL's foundation, consider three things. First, find that rock star—the strong teacher, curricular unit, or a community partner ready for the opportunity. Beginning with a stellar foundational piece goes a long way toward success. Second, don't bite off too much. Many educators are tempted to make the initial effort large-scale. Start small and manageable. Develop goals, write them down, and work to attain them. It is better to have a solid, small success than a weak, large failure. Third, talk it up. Publicly and privately showcase the effort and the partner's contributions. Everyone likes recognition and appreciation. The more educators recognize the community partner and show appreciation, the more likely the partner is to remain involved and speak positively about the school and district.

GET THE RIGHT PEOPLE ON THE BUS

One district had a school-community panel on CBL. The group included a retired guidance counselor who worked for the local chamber of commerce as a liaison between businesses and schools. This man's primary responsibility was to bridge the gap between what businesses want from students and the educational opportunities schools provide. The man, Cedric, had a jaded opinion of schools and educators, and believed that if teachers got out of the way, business people could show students what is important. He was very vocal with his opinion. When a group member explained the importance of building relationships and positive experiences, Cedric said, "Forget all that nonsense. Force teachers to work with at least one business partner every year as part of their contract. Bam! Just like that you would have 800 new partnerships."

Not every teacher in school is ready to advocate for a well-executed CBL partnership. Staff need time and professional development to gain expertise. Some undoubtedly are fully ready; others are prepared for parts of the process. And a few may not be ready for a long time. Cedric's focus was purely on the numbers: Zero partnerships is bad; 800 partnerships is good. He did not consider the quality of the partnership or the long-term damage that a failed experience could bring. In *Good to Great*, Jim Collins (2001a) writes that great leaders don't try to convince people of the direction they need to go. Collins suggests that leaders get the right people in place to create the necessary change. Cedric's energy could become a positive if leaders developed him as an asset by identifying and capitalizing on his strengths. If Cedric continues to be destructive or counterproductive, he may need to, in Collins's words, "get off the bus."

SOURCE YOUR CHAMPIONS

One difficulty in beginning to implement CBL is convincing district leaders to allocate resources. A Wisconsin high school petitioned its district for a CBL coordinator. The principal saw the need for someone to actively seek partnerships and work with students to track their individualized learning. The principal wanted someone to be a public advocate and a person who also knew curriculum and instruction well enough to not allow the experiences to stray from the core mission of education. Several candidates were qualified for the position, but the board resisted spending money on an untested plan.

A high school teacher named Sallie* volunteered as CBL coordinator. Sallie connected teachers to partners throughout the district and worked with students to track benchmarks and on independent curriculum mapping. When the team took their proposal for a CBL coordinator to the board for official approval, they were not the only voices at the table. Community partners and students attested to the importance of the position. After many questions, a review of supporting research, and a lot of discussion, the board approved the position. The position was posted, Sallie applied, and she was hired.

Someone has to be the face of the district to establish partnerships. A human connection makes or breaks partnership possibilities. Leaders need to support CBL with the resources necessary to establish those human connections.

Mathews (1996) contends that "school systems appear to be walled off as formal, quasi-governmental institutions rather than public agencies embedded in a rich civic network" (p. 19). CBL responds by enabling every educator to move the institution from isolation toward connection. By building relationships that transcend the walls of the respective organizations, schools and communities work together to improve society through common outcomes.

SHARED OUTCOMES

Woodridge State High School and the community of Queensland, Australia, shared a concern. The school was not meeting the needs of the culturally diverse student population, so in 2010, the school began fostering partnerships with the intent of creating a "shared vision to improve learning outcomes for students" (Queensland Government, 2013). The Pacific Links collaboration involves parents, students, educators, and community members working together to meet the needs of Polynesian students through mentoring, family engagement strategies, community focus groups, and interventions. The Queensland Government states, "Together, exceptional results have been achieved, including a 93 per cent improvement in attendance and behaviour for a core group of students. The model implemented at Woodridge State High School is now recognised as one of best practice" (Queensland Government, 2013).

Amy Clark and her husband Ryan helped found, run, and partially own a company in Washington called Liberty Bottle Works. They create artistic, American-made aluminum water bottles. Clark's daughter attended nearby Naches Valley Intermediate School where the arts program was in danger of being cut. Clark wanted to help keep arts alive at her daughter's school so she sprang into action, volunteering to teach art. At the end of the first year, students sold their works to support the program, and more local businesses joined the cause to see student art programs continue. Clark helped keep arts in school and students have a newfound passion for learning through art (Hilf, 2013).

CBL Link: Successful partnerships benefit partners as well as students. To get partners interested in CBL, educators help partners see the benefits—exposure for the organization and increased student success. Positive student outcomes are better for students, educators, organizations, and the community.

INCREASE INTENTIONALITY

Purposeful instruction works (Hattie, 2009, p. 164), but that doesn't mean everyone is doing it. Purposeful instruction is instruction based on clear goals and outcomes (i.e., standards based). Teachers select targets and take care and time to examine successes and areas for growth as they plan instruction.

Kim-Marie Cortez-Riggio is a fifth-grade teacher at Glenwood Landing Elementary School in Sea Cliff, New York, who wanted to help students reach English-language arts benchmarks and at the same time help them see that their work in the classroom could mean something to their community. She carefully planned out which community partners she wanted to engage, curricular benchmarks she wanted to meet, and ways to assess the experience (Cortez-Riggio, 2011). Because she was intentional, students developed their critical thinking skills in a way that was relevant to them and to the community. "I watched students transform their world through an environment-focused project and, in doing so, I learned that they also transformed themselves into critical thinkers and experienced speakers whose voices had become protectors of the Earth" (Cortez-Roggio, 2011, p. 39). Intentional focus behind actions gets results (Bereiter & Scardamalia, 1989).

SEEK TRANSFER

Successful planners observe what is around them and capitalize on what they find. Talking to people and asking questions can lead to ideas for connecting to community expertise. A village in the Canary Islands, for example, resurrected an ancient whistle language by teaching it in school (D'Amelio, 2012). This language does not exist beyond the island of La Gomera, but for the community, the language has history and enough meaning that the community felt it important to add to the school curriculum. A similar possibility exists in the small community of Pulaski, north of Green Bay, Wisconsin, which has a rich history of polka music. People in Pulaski perform polka music, speak the Polish language, cook Polish food, and dance the polka—it is their heritage. The schools in Pulaski have an opportunity to connect to their community and align cultural to benchmarks for learning. By watching for ideas for CBL, educators continuously improve opportunities for it to occur.

CUSTOMIZATION AND INDIVIDUALIZATION

Customizing education takes work and preparation to know each student, understand where each needs to progress, keep each one on track to be ready for assessments, and continually seek and grow new experiential learning opportunities. But that is educators' job.

The Wiggins and McTighe (2011) *Understanding by Design* framework challenges educators to ensure that students do not only acquire knowledge, but make meaning of it, and ultimately transfer that knowledge to new situations.

One tool to help educators customize CBL is a benchmark log. (A benchmark coach could help, but in times of scarce resources, the classroom teacher can make this tool work.) A benchmark log helps teachers play "on the edges of the box" rather than "outside the box." Chapter 4 described how the Community-Based Learning School teachers created their own units. Under pressure to stay within the curriculum, four teachers pulled apart the content, identified relevant themes, and aligned the approved curriculum to the themes. They stayed within the boundaries of the established curriculum but used vastly different instructional techniques. They danced on the edges of the box without going outside it. The challenge is to create a way to maintain the established curriculum but change delivery to a full CBL experience.

At one high school, CBL educators went through the regular curriculum in science, social studies, and English and identified the benchmarks they wanted students to meet. The benchmarks were identical to those taught in regular classes in the school. The teachers mapped out their year and created four curricular stopping points aligned with quarters to use a summative evaluation to ensure that all students were on track for end-of-the-year benchmarks. Table 5.1 shows this Benchmark Log. Throughout the four segments, teachers and the benchmark coach let students determine their own learning paths and guided them where they had gaps. By paying careful attention to student learning paths and by creating learning experiences that caused students to *want* to learn, in one year, 80% to 90% of the 75 students reached proficiency on the benchmarks (Dumke, personal communication, 2012).

EVALUATE CURRENT PARTNERSHIPS

Understanding current partnerships is a critical step in scaling partnerships up to the next level. What potential exists for a partner to improve the level of relationship to joint instruction or full CBL? Identifying potential can transform educators' practice.

Table 5.1   Benchmark Log

1- Minimal 2- Basic n/a Not Assessed 3- Proficient 4- Advanced	Martin	Jesus	Malachai	Angel	Kayla	Alexia
CCSS. ELA-Literacy.RST. 9-10.2 Determine the central ideas or conclusions of a text; trace the text's explanation or depiction of a complex process, phenomenon, or concept; provide an accurate summary of the text.	2.5	n/a	3	3.5	2.5	4
CCSS.ELA-Literacy.RST. 9-10.1 Cite specific textual evidence to support analysis of science and technical texts, attending to the precise details of explanations or descriptions.	3	3	2.5	n/a	3	3
CCSS.ELA-Literacy.RH.9-10.7 Integrate quantitative or technical analysis (e.g., charts, research data) with qualitative analysis in print or digital text.	n/a	2.5	4	3	n/a	3

SCALING UP PARTNERSHIPS

Opportunities for CBL are everywhere. Educators need to be on the lookout for situations like these:

A string of educational partnerships in Dallas, Texas, showed how a community wraparound system can develop through efforts to scale up a CBL project. Big Thought, a nonprofit organization in Dallas, Texas, that promotes educational innovation and community partnerships, began with local artists volunteering time in the public schools in 1987. A number of partnerships blossomed from there, including an at-risk program that involved collaboration with the Dallas County Juvenile Department and a preliteracy program in which the schools partnered with the Dallas Public Library. These collaborations led to a systemic partnership between the schools and the city called Thriving Minds, which is an initiative that developed a "system of neighborhood-based hubs" to ensure "that creative learning is everywhere children live and learn" (Bransom, Denson, Hoitsma, & Pinto, 2010). Their goal is to work with their more than 100 community partners to incorporate art and creativity into every Dallas school.

Over time, academic partnerships can be scaled up beyond CBL to create a community-wide collaborative system that supports students and their learning so that they become active and engaged citizens.

Table 5.2 Partnership Assessment Tool

This tool has been designed to assist the reader in identifying at which level a partnership exists. To use this assessment, first, list your partnership. Then reflect on the characteristics of that partnership to see where it best fits in this continuum. By completing this exercise, it will be easier to see the depth of the partnerships that exist, and will give readers an idea of where there is potential to "scale up" to the next level.

PARTNERSHIP CHARACTERISTICS	INFORMATION	COMMUNICATION	RELATIONSHIP	PARTNERSHIP	JOINT INSTRUCTION	COMMUNITY-BASED LEARNING
The school and partner are aware of one another.	X	X	X	X	X	X
The school and the partner communicate with one another.		X	X	X	X	X
The school and partner engage in non-curricular activities with one another.			X	X	X	X
The school and partner engage in curricular activities together.				X	X	X
The school or partner allows/encourages a specific curriculum to be taught in the other's setting.					X	X
The school and partner plan curricular experiences together.						X
The school and partner share accountability for curricular outcomes.						X
The school and partner collaboratively reflect on the partnership.						X
The partnership between the school and community increases advocacy between the two entities.						X

Table 5.2, Partnership Assessment Tool, is designed to help educators identify their existing partnership level. To review an existing partnership, read the descriptors in the first column and mark the category that best fits that partnership.

In every new endeavor it is important to know those practices that will help to ensure success. By tending to the important factors that facilitate CBL, educators increase the chances that their innovation will be successful.

Questions for Reflection

1. Where in our district are opportunities that will result in a "quick win"?
2. What educator in our setting might be an outstanding advocate for the district?
3. What curricular unit is appropriate and ready to incorporate a community partner?
4. Which community organizations/leaders might be ready to deepen their involvement with the school/district?

CHAPTER 6

Professional Development for Community– Based Learning

MAIN IDEA

Aligning best practices in professional learning with the best practice of community-based learning creates powerful instruction and community connection that will impact student learning.

Community-based learning (CBL) is situational and cannot be scripted. It requires thinking about and examining student, community, and educational needs. Educators who are serious about CBL must be equally serious about learning *how* to do CBL.

In schools, the amount of time teachers have for professional learning is often limited. For teachers to achieve system goals, professional learning must be linked to those goals (DuFour, 2004). If systemic implementation of CBL is a priority, leaders must plan professional development that advances its practice.

Thomas Guskey, an educational researcher whose expertise is professional development, establishes a framework to help educators develop effective professional learning practices. He advocates following five steps:

1. Establish student learning goals.

2. Determine the best practices to achieve those goals.

3. Identify the necessary resources (human, physical, and financial).

4. Decide what teachers need to know and be able to do.

5. Gain the knowledge and skills (Guskey, 2002).

Using this framework, educational leaders can plan systemic implementation of CBL.

1. ESTABLISH STUDENT LEARNING GOALS

CBL has clear student learning goals: Students achieve the curricular expectations aligned with the Common Core through project-based learning experiences that connect classroom to community. When practicing CBL, educators should envision a "T" chart, with the learning goals on one side and the corresponding community goals on the other. In a standards-based curriculum, attention is always given to the learning goal. In CBL, those learning goals are then matched with appropriate community outcomes to ensure simultaneous benefit to school and community.

2. DETERMINE THE BEST PRACTICES TO ACHIEVE THOSE GOALS

Advocates of curriculum integration maintain that it is highly successful (Beane, 1995; Hartzler, 2000; Vars, 1991). Hattie's (2009) meta-analysis of 61 studies on integrated curricula had a more moderate conclusion, finding a medium effect on student achievement. At the same time, Hattie's meta-analysis of 221 studies on problem-based teaching shows integrated curricula positively affect student achievement.

New York's International High School at LaGuardia Community College is an example of interdisciplinary success. The school is designed primarily to serve students who have been in the country for fewer than four years. Students meet graduation requirements by passing yearlong interdisciplinary programs that incorporate the humanities, math, science, technology, and applied learning (The International High School, 2013, para. 2). The school received an A on the 2011–12 state progress report and is in the 97th percentile of New York's schools for student achievement. Overall, student performance on the state progress report has increased from the 53rd percentile in 2010 to the 82nd percentile in 2012. The school's mission statement says:

> *Teams create curriculum, schedule students and teachers, develop strategies to support students, hire teachers, have a voice in shaping schoolwide policies and determine assessment procedures. This interdisciplinary structure has been responsible for improved student attendance and achievement.* (The International High School, 2013, para. 5)

While not a CBL interdisciplinary example, International High School does provide evidence of the success of the interdisciplinary approach.

When educators test educational strategies, they need to be confident that the strategy is well-researched and has a record of success. Research supports curriculum integration as an effective practice, and curriculum integration is necessary to practice CBL.

The Center on Organization and Restructuring of Schools in Madison, Wisconsin, conducted a five-year study of conditions needed to "make organizational innovations successful" (Newmann & Wehlage, 2005, para. 1). After studying more than 1,500 K–12 students across the United States, the center found that one key to successful innovation is authentic pedagogy.

> *The center developed a set of specific teaching standards that measure the extent to which students are challenged to think, to develop in-depth understanding, and to apply academic learning to important, real-world problems. These standards are called*

"Authentic Pedagogy." Our research showed that students who receive more authentic pedagogy learn more. (Newmann & Wehlage, 2005, para. 12)

If real-world problems (authentic pedagogy) lead to greater student learning and CBL uses authentic pedagogy, then it is reasonable to conclude that CBL is likely to improve student learning.

Teachers don't need a concrete plan to start CBL, but they do need a clear vision and mission. What gets measured gets done, so teachers must set goals to help achieve an overall mission and vision.

Peter Senge (1990), author of *The Fifth Discipline* and founder of the international professional learning community called the Society for Organizational Learning, defines vision as "an image of the future we seek to create" (p. 5). Mind Tools, a company established by business experts to help other businesses achieve their goals, defines a vision as a statement that "defines the organization's purpose . . . in terms of the organization's values" (1999, para. 4). According to educational historian Jamie Vollmer (2010), the purpose of school is to meet the needs of the community.

In CBL, "community" can be defined globally. The vision for CBL, then, is to equip students to function as contributing citizens to the global community. A vision should be that thing toward which people are constantly striving. It helps to keep focus.

Educators also need to develop a mission to formalize objectives. The mission strategically guides the organization's activities. The mission statement for CBL should closely align with the organization's vision. If the vision is to equip students to function as contributing citizens to the global community, what needs to be done to achieve that purpose? Likewise, if the vision is to assist students in fulfilling the needs in their local town, village, or city, then what needs to be done to achieve that goal?

The Common Core State Standards and P21 framework emphasize problem solving, communication, and technology. Educators also should match these demands to needs within their own communities. For example, a small Dutch community in Wisconsin feared the loss of their cultural heritage. Their primary evidence for this fear was the dwindling interest in the annual "Kermis" Dutch festival. Community leaders approached the local school to ask for help. The teachers in the school quickly found relevant curricular connections, primarily in social studies, language arts, art, and music. Through a partnership with the school, the Kermis festival was reenergized and the students learned the curricular material while learning about their heritage.

3. IDENTIFY THE NECESSARY RESOURCES

Professional development is "the process of improving staff skills and competencies needed to produce outstanding educational results for students," says Emily Hassel, codirector of an education policy and management firm (1999, p. 1). Professionals need to stay current with their practice or they risk losing their edge. Staying abreast of research and best practice makes sense. A surgeon who didn't stay abreast of current learning in the medical field wouldn't stay a surgeon much longer.

Research from the 2007 U.S. Department of Education Study examined more than 1,300 studies on professional development and found nine that showed direct evidence of professional development's effect on student achievement (Carpenter, Fennema, Peterson, Chiang, & Loef, 1989; Cole, 1989; Duffy et al., 1986; Marek & Methven, 1991; McCutchen et al., 2002; McGill-Franzen, Allington, Yokoi, & Brooks, 1999; Saxe, Gearhart, & Nasir, 2001; Sloan, 1993; Tienken, 2003). The synthesis of these studies showed that for professional development to be most successful it needs to be

- Extensive (49 hours on average for these nine studies)
- Ongoing (often presented in a main session with follow-up throughout the year)

Teachers say that the most valuable professional development is embedded, collaborative, and connected to goals (Post Primary Teachers' Association, 2013). When "drive-by interventions are replaced by longer-term designs, there is a greater chance that teachers will improve instruction," according to Jenny DelMonte, author of *High Quality Professional Development for Teachers* (2013, p. 7).

DelMonte (2013) outlines features of professional development as those that

- have a connection to organizational goals,
- address both the content and instructional strategies,
- contain active learning for teachers,
- allow for collaboration, and
- use "follow-up and continuous feedback" (p. 6).

Determine how you will procure the time, supplies, and people needed to develop ongoing, extensive professional development year-round, connected to your CBL goals.

The No Child Left Behind Act (Title IX, Part A, Sections 9101 (V) (I)) states that professional development should be "high-quality, sustained, intensive, and classroom-focused," and "not 1-day or short-term workshops or conferences."

The first factor to be considered in professional development for CBL, then, is time, and the second factor is method of delivery. Planners of CBL need to reserve time in the schedule to allow teachers to collaborate to develop CBL lessons, units, or even systems. Collaborative conversations often need to be facilitated to ensure the group develops into a professional learning community in which members focus on results and ultimately ensure that students learn (DuFour, 2004). Creative leaders manage time by looking at existing structures and asking,

- How can what we are currently doing be reorganized to facilitate professional conversations?
- What percentage of teachers' time is dedicated to discussions about learning?
- How can we increase that percentage?

One school district had 35 hours of professional development in the calendar. When district administrators examined the schedule, they realized that only about a third of those hours were spent discussing students and learning. They reprioritized, and the following year, more than 75% of educators' time was spent discussing students and learning. To ensure that CBL grows, administrators must find the time for teachers to share their experiences, explore new experiences, and connect those experiences to student outcomes.

Professional development sometimes consists of bringing in an expert for a day and then sending teachers back to their classrooms in the hope that they will have taken something useful from the presentation and use it in their classrooms. Embedding professional learning in teachers' work and workday is important to successfully transforming practice. The structure of the professional development must allow teachers to have ongoing conversations about the principles of CBL so they can examine the process, not just the product.

Money is always difficult to procure, but to make the case to allocate financial resources, planners can make decision makers aware of expenses in other areas. If administrators are strategic in their planning and create the conditions in which people are on board with the mission and vision behind CBL, then reallocating resources becomes much simpler.

An additional resource in community-based planning is, of course, the community partners. Planners ask,

- Where are those opportunities to connect with the community?
- With whom do we have a relationship?
- With whom can we start one?
- How deep are existing relationships? Where are the opportunities to scale up?
- Can we develop a person to take on the role of networking with and establishing partners? Whether it is an extra duty, a volunteer position, or a full-time position, hiring a CBL coordinator can maximize partnership opportunities in a very purposeful way. And if done right, the community may turn around and support the district financially when it is most needed.

4. DECIDE WHAT TEACHERS NEED TO KNOW AND BE ABLE TO DO

When practiced with fidelity, CBL uses an integrated curriculum in which students achieve learning targets using real-world experiences. Real-world tasks do not occur in neat subject areas. Content overlaps. To shift instructional practices, however, requires that teachers integrate subject areas. James Beane, a researcher and advocate of an integrated curriculum, states:

> *Curriculum integration begins with the idea that the sources of curriculum ought to be problems, issues, and concerns posted by life itself . . . . Since life itself does not know the boundaries or compartments of what we call disciplines of knowledge, such a context uses knowledge in ways that are integrated.* (Beane, 1995, p. 616)

Teachers have options for the sometimes challenging task of delivering interdisciplinary instruction. Drake and Burns (2004) suggest three categories for interdisciplinary teaching.

- Multidisciplinary: A group of teachers work together to teach within their own subject areas but teach around an established theme.
- Interdisciplinary: Teachers revise the curriculum to combine subject areas so that subjects are less identifiable.
- Transdisciplinary: The curriculum is completely merged and centers on student contexts as described by Beane (1995) earlier.

Curriculum integration allows teachers to teach the curriculum with distinct subject areas in mind, but without having subjects define the lesson's content. Instead, content is connected to real situations because lessons recognize the connections among the disciplines. Teachers help students connect their learning to their community and world. Because real problems generally are not isolated by a content area but are complex and cross numerous disciplines, CBL addresses the curriculum in a more relevant way. Educators may find real-world situations limited to a single subject, but such experiences seldom require the deep, meaningful thinking that CBL is designed to elicit.

Vars (1991) offers three approaches to integrating curriculum to fit into CBL:

- All the school's teachers agree on a theme and all teach to it for an extended period.
- In an interdisciplinary team approach, "teachers of several different subjects are assigned one group of students and

encouraged to correlate at least some of their teaching" (Vars, 1991, p. 14).
- Teachers use a block-time and self-contained class, as in elementary school, with a single educator teaching several subjects within that block of time.

With varied approaches to the curriculum, schools can select the one most appropriate for their degree of readiness to improve the chances of successful implementation.

Another challenge to implementation can be teachers' readiness for more change. Most states have adopted the Common Core State Standards. When many districts are heavily invested in standards-based learning, how does curriculum integration work? Gordon Vars and James Beane (2000) point educators to researchers and practitioners who have dissected the subject areas to create what they call "common learnings" (Vars & Beane, 2000, para. 6).

The National Alliance for School Reform (NASR) and the Center for Occupational Research and Development (CORD) have studied curriculum using a world rather than subject lens. They work backward to identify content area standards that align to real-world problems. Educators can use NASR's or CORD's work, or they can create units themselves.

Teachers need to plan relevant learning experiences. To deepen learning experiences and allow students to make meaning of their learning, teachers need to build expertise in instructional methods for teaching an integrated curriculum. Understanding how subject areas work together is crucial to understanding the real-world application necessary to engage in CBL.

SCALING UP AN INTEGRATED CURRICULUM PROJECT

Elena Aguilar (2008), a teacher in Oakland, California, described how an integrated curriculum helped students make connections in her classroom. Science students studied the physiological and social implications of HIV/AIDS. When the English lesson focused on the plague in 14th century Europe, students immediately drew connections to their science classwork. Aguilar followed the students' lead and continued the integration. The challenge in this example of curriculum integration is scaling up the opportunity for integration.

(Continued)

(Continued)

Scaling Up: The teacher might consider who in the community could be called upon to lend expertise to the curricular planning and instruction. Doctors and others in health-related fields are obvious choices. Other possibilities include those have been personally affected by these diseases, university professors who have studied the phenomena, local librarians or historians, and advocates for a cure. In this case, the school has a strong curricular unit that could lend itself to a CBL partnership. Identifying these units is an appropriate initial step in creating CBL.

5. GAIN THE KNOWLEDGE AND SKILLS

"[New learning is] necessary to challenge existing assumptions and develop the kinds of new knowledge and skills associated with positive outcomes for students," according to Helen Timperley of the International Bureau of Education (2008, p. 20). The previous section outlined areas where teachers need professional learning to successfully accomplish CBL. The final portion of Guskey's framework requires actions aligned to those areas. These activities should be considered:

Research

Teachers need to spend time learning about CBL. Practitioners can review books and articles about CBL examples, as well as about pedagogical skills to support practice. Principals also can find relevant videos and online resources to share with teachers. Within the professional learning community, research and the accompanying discussion increases knowledge of practice and allows educators to begin to plan and refine the CBL experience.

Develop Community Relations Skills

Interacting with stakeholders is critically important in any organization (Epstein, 1995; Paine & McCann, 2009; Sanders, 2006; Schneider & Hollengzer, 2006). Educators typically don't study communication skills. When an educator speaks, like it or not, what they say influences how people feel about the educational institution for which the teacher works. Teachers who are aware of the power of their words and actions have the opportunity to intentionally support and improve community relations. Educators must also understand how to better determine the needs of their customers—community partners (Lawrimore, 2011). Training on how to identify and achieve mutual goals is a part of a CBL professional development plan. A two-hour session on customer service can be helpful. Teachers who view the community as one of their customers and work to meet community needs as they are meeting student needs build capacity for CBL.

AN INVOLVED PUBLIC IS A SUPPORTIVE PUBLIC

The Greater Beloit Economic Development Corporation (GBEDC) in Beloit, Wisconsin, was developed in 2005 to "propel competitive and prosperous growth throughout the region" (Greater Beloit Economic Development Corporation, 2012, p. 1). Its primary role is to collaborate with area businesses to develop and maintain employment opportunities in the community. As part of this mission, the GBEDC understood the importance of strong schools to economic development, and the organization made a commitment to support local schools "with volunteer efforts, funds, and business-to-education initiatives" (Greater Beloit Works, 2012, p. 1). In 2012, GBEDC's commitment to the School District of Beloit was put to the test when the district presented the community with a $70 million facilities referendum. If the referendum passed, the district would rebuild/expand several schools, update the swimming pool, and add tennis courts (School District of Beloit, 2012). When the district began promoting the referendum, the GBEDC released a statement of full and unanimous support for the endeavor. Possibly as a result, the referendum passed in March 2012, and the School District of Beloit is working through its three-phase facilities plan.

CBL Link: If community partners see the value schools bring to the community, they are more likely to support schools' needs with human, physical, and financial resources. Be proactive in involving community partners.

Bring in the Experts

Many people understand and engage in CBL, if not in its entirety, at least in some components. Many of these educators are willing to speak to other teachers or even work with them through embedded professional development. Bringing in an outside expert can help educators see beyond what they know to explore new and different possibilities (Timperley, 2008).

Visit Schools for Examples

CBL and related practices are occurring everywhere. After discovering a relevant exemplar, teachers may consider a site visit. Seeing something gives people a different perspective than reading or hearing about it. A site visit also allows educators to see teachers and students actually engaging in the experience. Experts can be very beneficial, but sometimes they are not engaging in the actual work. Speaking to those who are practicing elements of CBL can be powerful.

Experiment

Education researcher Robert Marzano (1992) outlines three phases of learning: the cognitive phase, the shaping phase, and the autonomous phase. To improve teaching CBL, teachers need to practice. Once they learn the strategy (cognitive phase), they need to try it out. They will make mistakes and refine the practice as they go (shaping phase), but once they are good at it, they will be able to practice it efficiently and effectively (autonomous phase).

Reflect and Collaborate

Professional learning is more powerful when it occurs within professional learning communities that promote collaboration, discussion, and reflection (Danielson & McGreal, 2000; DuFour, 2004; Hargreaves & Fullan, 1992).

CBL NEEDS DEVELOPMENT

Researchers Anne Henderson and Karen Mapp (2002), who synthesized the findings of 51 empirical studies to establish the effect that family and community involvement has on student achievement, found that "effective programs to engage families and community embrace a philosophy of partnership. The responsibility for children's educational development is a collaborative enterprise among parents, school staff, and community members" (p. 51). They write, "Parent and community involvement that is linked to student learning has a greater effect on achievement than more general forms of involvement" (p. 38).

Connecting with stakeholders in a meaningful way that is linked to student achievement is critical for schools. To successfully engage in CBL, teachers need time to learn new ways to integrate curriculum and to collaborate around planning and the effort. They need to learn communication skills and to connect with potential partners. All of this is a continuous, ongoing effort to improve student achievement.

Questions for Reflection

1. How is our professional development time organized to support systemic learning around the areas of greatest importance in our school/district?
2. How do our current educational structures promote or inhibit the practices necessary to implement CBL?
3. In which areas do we see the greatest need for professional development to develop, implement, and support CBL?
   - Establishing a mission and vision?
   - Appropriate instructional practices?
   - Effectively engaging the community?

CHAPTER 7

Leading
Community–
Based Learning

MAIN IDEA

Leaders need to make personal connections to constantly push others' thinking toward community-based learning and to maximize the capacity of those willing to attempt the strategy.

"Who of you is comfortable calling yourself a leader?" In his 2010 TEDTalk (http://www.ted.com/talks/drew_dudley_everyday_leadership.html), Drew Dudley tells the story of the day he handed out lollipops at a college orientation. A girl who was nervous about going to college was ready to tell her parents that college life wasn't for her. Dudley handed a lollipop to a young man and told the young man to give the lollipop to the most beautiful woman in the world. The young man, now bright red with embarrassment, gave the lollipop to the girl standing next to him—the same girl who was so nervous. She stayed in school, and the two are now married. Dudley himself does not recall the incident and was told later of the impact of his action. He uses the story to illustrate

85

what he terms "lollipop moments," saying that leadership is not grandiose but can be a small, everyday moment that occurs spontaneously. As a leader, how are you looking at large and small opportunities to make a difference?

Facilitating community-based learning (CBL) requires applying leadership theories. CBL can affect the system, but it also can be someone's lollipop moment. A leader breaks "patterns of accepted modes of thought and action" (Kirton, 1976, p. 623). Innovative leaders cultivate tolerance for risk, perseverance, clarity on social responsibility, and a growth mind-set (Dweck, 2006).

RESPONDING TO THE NEED FOR HIGH QUALITY

The perceived failure of public education is a failure of leadership. When people do not know what to do next, they do what they have always done (Neal, Wood, & Drolet, 2013). CBL demands innovation, not just adaptation. CBL allows leaders to strengthen ties with the community while increasing relevance for students and refining educator practice. CBL can start small and build to create an educational setting that is fundamentally different than traditional education. It raises the bar on the standard of expectation for students, teachers, and community and leaves a leadership legacy.

A TOLERANCE FOR RISK

When a district has one or two successful CBL experiences, educators might be tempted to be satisfied with good. "We had two good partnerships last year! We are amazing!" That may be true, but "good is the mortal enemy of great" (Collins, 2012, track 1). Leaders can be satisfied with one or two CBL partnerships, or they can press forward to transform an organization. Transforming a system and its entities takes time, patience, and often resources. The leadership challenge is to continue the quest toward greatness. What does a leader do and expect? The leader capitalizes on energy from early adopters to sustain the change.

One elementary school built on an early adopters' energy. A manufacturer had partnered with the fifth-grader teacher for an extended CBL experience. When the experience was over, district leaders sprang into action. They invited managers at the manufacturing plant to a televised board meeting to present the activity. They publicly praised the company employees for their contribution, and they publicly committed to a long-term relationship. The superintendent nominated the manufacturing company for local awards that celebrated community partnerships. Students, teachers, principals, and district administrators wrote personal thank-you notes to those involved in the experience. The recognition, along with the high quality of the experience, caused this partner to continue to want to work with the schools and made the community partner an advocate for the school. The company managers spoke positively about their experiences, and other community partners became intrigued with helping the schools. Education leaders must capitalize on the power of recognition.

Once people are excited about the idea of CBL and have successful examples, new leadership challenges arise. As more partners and educators seek to be involved, professional development needs arise. Consider local educators. How equipped are they to be effective ambassadors for your building? It will take time to cultivate their potential.

At the end of a CBL planning session with a local business partner, one teacher remarked, "Well, now all that is left is for you to come and try to do our job. You think teaching is so easy, and now you are about to find out the truth." Thankfully an administrator was there to rescue the conversation. The administrator pointed out that whenever people enter an unfamiliar realm, they experience new challenges and that teachers would be there to help and work with the partners to make the experience successful.

Leaders need to take time to work with staff to understand what it means to be an ambassador. Role-playing, written resources, and even expert presenters can help. When leaders set a high expectation, they must offer staff support in order for the initiative to succeed. This holds true not only for the public relations aspect of CBL but also for planning the curriculum, recognitions, and assessments.

Support is critical to sustain CBL, but equally critical is a balance of pressure. While policy isn't necessary to practice CBL, leaders can accelerate the practice by setting policy and district-level goals that align preK–12. "Systemization" does not necessarily mean "linear and sequential." Districts can set lofty goals, but until those goals reach the classroom, they mean nothing. In one school a teacher asked, "Do you mean to tell me that my personal goal has to relate to the school goal?" The answer was an unequivocal, "Yes!"

Richard DuFour advocates leadership that fosters autonomy and creativity (loose) within a systematic framework that stipulates clear, nondiscretionary priorities, and parameters (tight) at the district level (DuFour, 2007). DuFour makes the case for selectively imposing top-down leadership and suggests that district leaders can and should invite input from professionals across the district. However, the directive to form effective professional learning communities across the district falls into the category of "tight"; for example, forming professional learning communities is nonnegotiable. Community engagement also must be district-driven and nonnegotiable.

A district may set a goal of increasing curricular community partnerships to improve community relations. A principal might then set a building goal of increasing curricular community partnerships so that students have more relevant learning experiences. The teacher then might write as a goal to develop two new curricular community partnerships within a year. This is systems thinking. It isn't top down. There is influence from the top, but the work and action happens at the ground level—in the classroom.

SITUATIONAL LEADERSHIP

No matter how large the scale of implementation for CBL is, leaders will be challenged to implement it. Transforming the system requires situational leadership (Blanchard & Johnson, 2003). Yukl (2006) defines situational leadership as "adapting to unpredictable events in the environment" (p. 159). CBL has to work within an individual setting, with that community's goals in mind.

The perfect experience for a rural Iowa school might involve an agricultural partnership, while a CBL experience in Los Angeles, California, might involve a partner from the entertainment industry. A community that wants to see students become skilled in vocations will have vastly different partners than a community that desires 21st century learning. Some schools have exceptional community partnerships but lack relevant student learning experiences. Other schools find that teachers don't want to become involved with community partners. Each district or school needs to adjust the CBL model and transfer the outlined concepts to what works in the local setting.

DISTRIBUTIVE LEADERSHIP

Richard Elmore (2000) states that distributed leadership "derives from the fact that large-scale improvement requires concerted action among people with different areas of expertise and a mutual respect that stems from an appreciation of the knowledge and skill requirements of different roles" (pp. 35–36).

An individual can lead CBL, but if an administrator wants to create systemwide change with this idea, one leader cannot do the work alone. "Community" is the essence of CBL. When CBL becomes a school goal and staff are not eager to participate, leaders may be tempted to carry on alone. A lone effort may improve a single classroom, but the system may not change since only a single educator is engaging in the process. That single educator can be the start of a systemic change if leaders build the entire staff's capacity, support them with professional development and resources, and empower them to be change agents. As staff become fluent in CBL, leaders can gradually engage the staff until they fully buy in and take on CBL themselves.

Bob Orvis, founder of the improvisational troupe Comedy Sports, does an improvisation routine in leadership training called "High Status, Low Status." He gives audience volunteers a scenario to act out, asking them to achieve high status in the group. Volunteers typically speak loudly and become more commanding. When Orvis reverses the activity and asks volunteers to achieve low status, they become meek and quiet. He then points out that neither approach is productive. A leader cannot overtly command power nor be falsely humble. The leader supports each individual so that the overall organization can succeed (Spillane, Halverson, & Diamond, 2001). Orvis says that if no one knows who is the boss, the leader has done a good job.

In community-based leadership, the leader succeeds by developing teachers as ambassadors for the school, students as

A SINGLE EDUCATOR CAN DO THIS WORK . . .

In Kimberly, Wisconsin, science teacher Eric Vander Loop had an idea. Vander Loop is passionate about the outdoors, and he wanted to share that passion with his students. He pitched the idea for a summer school class called "river studies." Elementary students would research local rivers and their environmental impact, and Vander Loop would take them to local rivers to fish, experiment, and hike. The idea was well received, but the budget was tight. Vander Loop sought community support. He contacted a relative who worked at Gander Mountain. The store supported the project with discounts and some donations, recognizing that these students could grow up to be more passionate about the outdoors and potential customers of their outdoor-focused merchandise. Vander Loop was able to offer the students a richer experience through this assistance, and enrollment in the class grew each year. One teacher alone created and sustained a CBL partnership.

. . . Or it can be systemic

U.S. Education Secretary Arne Duncan organized the Ariel Community Academy when he was with Chicago Public Schools, in collaboration with John Rogers of Ariel Investments, LLC. In the Academy, each grade level received $20,000 to invest in first grade (two classes at $10,000 each). The funds are managed for them in a Charles Schwab account until fourth grade, when students start to pick stocks under the supervision and guidance of the classroom investment teacher. Upon graduation, the students reendow the $20,000 to the incoming first grade class. Then they use half of their profits to make a charitable gift to an entity of their choice. The other half is divided among the students, who have the option to cash out their share or deposit it into a 401k and have their funds matched with $1,000 provided by Ariel investments. In an *Edutopia* video (Ellis, 2003), narrator Kris Welch explains that each child receives about $100 to invest. The partnership aims to teach math skills through project-based learning, but the students also learn valuable lessons about collaboration, communication, and community support. The partnership was formed with a mission to provide a solid base of financial literacy to the students and their families through real-world, real-time learning.

   CBL Link: CBL can be a single experience or a whole instructional framework. The key is selecting an appropriate level of involvement for the local context. Find educators passionate about the idea, capitalize on their enthusiasm, and ideas can grow into meaningful learning opportunities.

self-directed and high-level learners, and community partners as school advocates. Community-based leadership is their moment to shine. The leader's moment is seeing the legacy of sustained community advocacy and student achievement.

MINDFUL LEADERSHIP

Leaders who attend a conference outside their district or state, or even out of the country, often spend two or three days being energized by new ideas and expertise and come back to school refreshed and ready to start a new initiative. Teachers comment, "We can always tell when our principal comes back from a conference because we have to start the next new thing." Renewed enthusiasm can be a wonderful impetus for needed change, but it can also cause staff to feel as though change is taking place around them instead of with them. Leaders need to recognize and meet people where they are to move individuals to create collective movement (Dickmann & Stanford-Blair, 2009).

Jim, an experienced business executive, often says, "Nothing happens in meetings." Leaders plan effectively and then allow people to move from meetings to action. Do you remember a time when you heard a good idea in a meeting and walked away thinking, "Now, how am I going to do that?" Approaching CBL with a large group helps define it, but bringing the experience to fruition requires one-on-one interactions with those involved. District administrators need to have discussions with principals. Principals need to have personal conversations with teachers. These conversations begin with assessing current practice, brainstorming possibilities, and selecting a course of action.

Rick was a highly motivated, traditional, high school social studies teacher who wanted to create more relevant learning experiences for his students. He asked his principal, "If I don't tell it to them, how are they going to learn it?" The principal gave him articles on relevant learning experiences and met with him regularly to challenge his thinking and practice, asking:

- What would happen if you tried that strategy?
- What does failure look like? Can that failure be productive?
- What does success look like?

- How are the students better off if you teach like you always have?
- What happens to student learning if you try teaching differently?
- How could you incorporate this small idea into your teaching, without making it feel burdensome?

The principal encouraged experimentation and starting small. Rick took small, calculated risks throughout the year, and at the beginning of the following year he asked the superintendent if he could plan a whole school around CBL. Through conversation, Rick's principal was able to determine his fears and reluctance and then tailor professional development to meet Rick's needs. The principal built trust with Rick and in the CBL concept. The principal became a valuable resource and support for Rick. Building trust is a critical but challenging task (Shaw, 1997). For CBL to succeed, a school or district must understand its core mission and how CBL relates to it. CBL's core tenets are as follows:

- Learning should be relevant to students.
- Teachers should guide the learning process to help students become passionate learners.
- Community organizations and educators work together to organize learning experiences that show how content knowledge applies in real-world settings.

Once this foundation is established and stakeholders understand it, convincing them that CBL is appropriate will be easier. Understanding "why" creates trust around the process.

SYSTEMS IMPLEMENTATION

When you are in Green Bay, Wisconsin, you know you are in Packer territory. Green and gold fences scatter the landscape, community members raffle donated Packer memorabilia, businesses have Packer dress-up days, players star in commercials and visit schools, people purchase nondividend earning stock just to be a part of the organization, Vince Lombardi is quoted in regular conversations, and every restaurant seems to incorporate some Packer memorabilia.

The Packers are the only NFL team owned by the community rather than a private owner. The Packers organization is proud of its role in the community and has created a culture. When people are in your district or school, is it obvious what you stand for? If you are serious about making CBL a systemic goal, people should know the moment they enter your district that it is a priority. Just as the Packers have created an obvious football culture in Green Bay, educators need to create an obvious CBL culture in their district.

Creating a CBL culture requires planning and intentionality. If CBL is your vision, then CBL should be part of your school improvement goal. Naming something as a priority, putting it on paper, and regularly communicating it makes that priority more likely to receive attention and be cultivated.

Those not ready to begin CBL can plant the seeds of the concept in a school improvement plan, perhaps using one of the following goals:

- Collaboratively plan a minimum of one lesson with a community partner.
- Investigate and create a list of potential community partners.
- Brainstorm current units and match with potential partners.
- Investigate and experiment with project based learning.

Whatever you choose to emphasize, build the foundation by helping staff understand why this method is important, and set incremental benchmarks to reach the goal.

Green Bay residents did not erect fences so that they could paint them green and gold. They had fences, and when they needed to paint them, they showed their team spirit by painting the fences in team colors. Community-based leadership is fresh paint on an existing framework. Teachers deliver instruction differently, but once the practice is honed, it becomes second nature and should not increase a teacher's workload.

For example, Carol was a third-grade teacher whose lessons with cars engaged her students. The third graders made an automobile "wish list," spent weeks researching cars (building literacy), created charts that included automobile features, and selected their "dream car" based on the information they found (demonstrating analysis and problem-solving). Carol then worked with the students to identify additional information, including fuel efficiency, emissions, and cost (developing math skills). Some students were so excited about the project that they asked their parents to take them to a dealership to pretend to shop for a new car so that they could see the car they chose in person. Next time she does this lesson, Carol could include a local car dealership owner who might appreciate an opportunity to share expertise and get future customers excited about automobiles. Students and teacher alike would gain from the dealer's expertise. If the teacher plans carefully and respects what the community leader could offer, the dealer would have a new understanding of the district's education. If Carol involved a community partner in planning and teaching the unit, she would have another adult, someone with expertise, helping to teach the students. CBL enhances these types of curricular experiences and uses them as catalysts to build community partnerships. A keen principal watching for opportunities could help Carol see the possibilities within her existing work.

Leaders trying to systematically implement CBL need to repeat the message incessantly. Mark Murphy, the president and CEO of the Green Bay Packers, doesn't miss an opportunity to praise the Green Bay community and say how integral the Packers are to that community. Packer fever is catching. Even when the team isn't doing well, people are proud to be a part of the community that has this organization. As an educational leader, never miss an opportunity to communicate the goals of CBL. Strong messages are benchmarked against high-achieving organizations rather than the school 12 miles down the road against which one can say, "We're good enough." Whether speaking with boards of education, chambers of commerce, district office, teachers, or students, CBL should be embedded into the conversation.

Consistent messaging is an art that takes practice and careful listening. When someone laments the lack of community support, decline in student engagement, or low teacher morale, leaders must be ready to tout the increased engagement and relevance found through CBL. When community members want more from graduates and complain that students are too wrapped up in technology to understand how to be a team member, leaders remind them that CBL fosters 21st century skills. When people say they want to help but don't know how to get involved, the reply is, "Through CBL." Advocacy will sustain the practice through the normal plateaus of change.

Researchers including Mavis Sanders (2006) and E. Joseph Schneider and Lara Hollengzer (2006) point out the importance of school-community relations. Their work has become fundamental to school leadership programs nationally, giving leaders a common vocabulary and outlining approaches to building community relationships.

As time becomes an increasingly valuable commodity, educators must change their practice. Maximizing leadership presence is crucial to success, but leaders no longer can spend hours at community meetings. Rather than the community knowing a person, community members need to know the schools as a community institution. For that change to occur, the community needs to become involved. The leader's time is better spent cultivating community-based learning experiences than working the crowd. The leader alone does not have the manpower to reach everyone. Rather than attending each individual fundraiser, the school leader can focus energy on networking with leaders of community organizations to help pave the road for curricular partnerships. By practicing networking at the 10,000-foot level instead of in the minutiae of events, school leaders can maximize their ability to reach numerous organizations. People may not love schools, but they love *their* school. They may not speak highly of teachers, but they love *their* teacher. Educators' job is to help people understand that schools are a collection of amazing individuals. By increasing their involvement in positive curricular experiences, we generate better community relations than a hundred speeches at community events.

The leader's role cannot be underestimated. What may seem like a small act to the leader may be someone else's lollipop moment. Leaders who understand their foundation and direction, who adapt and change as context necessitates, and who stay the course in the face of resistance become the catalyst through which change occurs.

Questions for Reflection

1. How does my leadership style align to CBL and the skills needed to facilitate implementation?
2. What ability do I have to foster change in my setting? Does my ability extend beyond my formal role? How can I leverage my leadership capacity to begin the practices?
3. How can individuals' strengths be used to lead CBL?

CHAPTER 8

Overcoming Barriers

MAIN IDEA

Every innovative change encounters barriers, including naysayers and those who attempt to find the easiest pathway rather than accomplishing the deep, meaningful work necessary to sustain a new practice.

In March 2013, Jeanne Moos, a reporter on CNN's *The Situation Room*, showed a viral video of a woman named Jessica Powell who was attached to a rope and standing on the edge of a cliff hundreds of feet high. Her plan was to "rope swing," jump off the cliff and swing freely in the air. Jessica was worried that she wouldn't be able to jump, though. When it was her turn, she stood on the edge of the cliff, terrified. Nothing could get her to jump. Her friends tried a countdown: "3—2—1!" Nothing. They coaxed her and pleaded. After 45 minutes, her boyfriend sidled up next to her and pushed her off. As she careened over the edge of the cliff she yelled, "I'm breaking up with you!" Viewers found out that Jessica was not only grateful for the push but had *asked* her boyfriend to push her if she tried to back out.

When it·comes to change and leaping into the unknown, like Jessica, people can sometimes get in their own way. Something that seems like a good idea, when someone comes to the edge, can seem like an impossible leap. Educators may put up many barriers to implementing community-based learning (CBL) and may need a nudge to jump in. Among the challenges are time, the pressure of standardized tests, risk aversion, problems with partners, feeling the need to "wait for the right time," toxic leaders, detractors, existing structures, and wants rather than needs.

TIME

Many states now mandate accountability measures of educator effectiveness. They have added Common Core State Standards and related assessments. Technology continues to change rapidly. And educators are expected to keep up with these changes and respond to changing student needs with individualized instruction. How can they take on another initiative?

CBL should not be approached as an initiative. CBL is an instructional strategy that changes how teachers teach. When teachers learn to implement this strategy well, they are able to go deeper into the curriculum and meet the expectations of the Common Core. They plan *differently*, not *more.*

A group of elementary teachers in the Southwest wanted to explore CBL. Teachers had designed units and had partners on board. The one piece they struggled with was assessments. The prior year's assessments tested students' ability to recall basic knowledge. The CBL experiences were going to elicit higher-order thinking from students.

These teachers needed to develop and use assessments matched to their instruction and learning goals. They were finding it difficult to step away from the unit assessments they were used to. They changed their instructional method and the level of learning they expected of students, but they wanted to keep their old assessments. After a great deal of collaboration and some nudging from their principal, the teachers created a new assessment that measured the appropriate targets.

The distinction between "more" and "different" is important. Educators may need time upfront in order to realize overall efficiency. Leaders need to have purposeful conversations to help educators let go of what they have always done and move into something new. When people don't know what to do next, they return to what they have always done. This fact leads to the well-known "implementation dip." CBL will seem hard at some point, and teachers will want to return to what seems easier from their past practice. What is efficient for adults is not necessarily best for children. Creating supports for CBL will help educators stay on track, brainstorm ideas, and let go of the old as they emerge into the new.

- Allow time to plan and collaborate.
- Find books, articles, and people that discuss CBL and how it works.
- Find places successfully engaging in CBL and arrange to visit.
- Develop professional learning communities around CBL.
- Cultivate a culture of informed risk-taking and innovation.

MAKING TIME

Once skilled in practicing CBL, educators are able to simultaneously engage students and the community.

Two schools in the Central Berkshire Regional School District in Dalton, Massachusetts, became Innovation Schools under 2010 state legislation. According to the Executive Office of Education for the state of Massachusetts, this legislation gave schools that chose to become Innovation Schools more flexibility and autonomy in most areas. Becket Washington Elementary embraced innovation with a goal of integrating communication and technology and also developed community partnerships. The school now works with numerous local art centers, festivals, and environmental groups to enhance student learning. Students have renewed interest in their education, and the district's innovation plan explicitly empowers teachers to innovate (Blake-Davis, 2012) The school continues to grow their innovation practices (Smith, 2013).

Two universities, St. Lawrence in Canton and Clarkson in Potsdam, New York, are partnering with a nearby school district to work with students to teach science, technology, engineering, and math classes in a project-based setting. University students have opportunities to practice teaching skills while earning credits, and the K–12 students benefit from engaging delivery of the content that shows them real-life applications for what they are learning. Clarkson University also states that "In addition, local teachers can update their

(Continued)

(Continued)
knowledge of the subject and form a better understanding of project-based learning"(Clarkson University, 2012).

The Kellogg Company is well known for its breakfast products. In Denton, Texas, the company partnered with schools to benefit students and break down a significant learning barrier: hunger. Kellogg's provided breakfast for nearly 350 Hodge Elementary School students who come to school hungry in the morning. The school allowed the Kellogg Company to create a video about the program to showcase the collaboration (Diggs, 2013). The result is good publicity for the company and students who begin their day fed and so are better prepared to learn (Tabor, 2013).

LARGE-SCALE TESTS

Educators feel pressured to focus on high-stakes tests. Most would rather have engaged students who learn as much as time allows than to cover all the material but have unengaged students. There are obviously degrees within these two extremes, but teachers are often put in a position where they must choose to lean toward depth or breadth of content. The Common Core is urging educators to focus on learning versus teaching, to go deeper into the content instead of wider. Students cannot simply acquire knowledge, but must be able to use that knowledge in new situations. Assessments are beginning to measure this transfer more successfully. When educators use strategies like CBL that involve students in solving problems, reacting to new information, hypothesizing, providing evidence for arguments, thinking critically, and collaborating, they foster true learning that helps students become able to use their knowledge under different circumstances. Educators who claim that the demands of standardized tests mean they cannot afford to engage in CBL do not understand the costs of not doing so.

RISK AVERSION

Wisconsin implemented a new educator evaluation system beginning in 2014–15. Student test scores will be one factor used to determine an educator's effectiveness. The change is likely to affect innovation in education.

An online article in the *Wausau* (Wisconsin) *Daily Herald* (Uhlig, 2013) about the inconsistent practices surrounding principal evaluation included links to approximately 25 principals' evaluations. Wisconsin's open records laws allow the public release of this information. Educators around the state reacted to the release with alarm. If principal evaluations are open records, they asked, could teacher evaluations also be open?

The new system will catalogue areas for improvement for educators. Teachers may not be willing to innovate and risk failure if they know that the information has a chance of being seen publicly. As Wisconsin Department of Public Instruction staff work out the details of the new evaluations, they are considering these confidentiality issues along with the goal of encouraging educators to improve their professional practice.

To best support improvement, educators must incorporate practices like CBL into the evaluation structure. Recent models of evaluation define high-quality teaching with many of the concepts necessary to engage in CBL: student engagement, student-led instruction, and collaboration (Danielson, 2013). Mayer-Mihalski and DeLuca (2009) state, "A combination of interactive tactics such as problem-based learning and simulation, along with reinforcement strategies such as 'commitment to change' instruments and follow-up reminders, must be incorporated into the design of educational programs in order to successfully change [teacher] behavior." Most evaluators focus on evaluating and coaching for these and other high-quality teaching methods in their evaluation practices. Evaluation and coaching are often connected to a school goal. If the goal is CBL, then CBL needs to be incorporated into the evaluation to better ensure success. By recognizing the practice as a goal, teachers can be coached and evaluated on the constructs of good teaching and the district's desired outcomes—in this case, CBL.

Another strategy that fosters innovation involves using data. Society currently relies on large-scale assessments to define learning and the factors that lead to educational success. Educators can offer the public an alternative. Many states have begun to incorporate student learning objectives to better measure outcomes, but even those objectives have become high stakes. High-quality assessments that focus on understanding and transfer lead to high-quality instruction (Wiggins & McTighe, 2011).

Creating classroom and unit assessments is a common practice in education. Through formative and summative assessments, educators can see student progress over the span of a unit instead of what is tested only during the testing window on a specific day. The new challenge is to ensure that these assessments align with Common Core expectations. Using carefully constructed assessments to measure higher-order thinking skills that CBL fosters, districts can use this new data source to triangulate with current assessments.

Taking a calculated risk is sometimes challenging for those working in the public eye. After facilitating new practices in CBL evaluation and assessment, administrators should consider how to communicate these practices to the public. When community members are educated on the importance and rigor of an educational strategy, their knowledge of the innovative practices better allows for innovation to take place.

PARTNERSHIP PERIL

A school district on the East Coast claimed to have well-established partnerships in its elementary schools. In actuality, partners were present in the classroom, but these partners instructed students while teachers sat in the back of the room and prepared for other classes. Were the partners engaged in the school? Yes, they were. Did the partnerships expand students' horizons and increase engagement? For the most part, yes. Did the partners leave with a better understanding of educators' work? Probably not. They likely understood what it feels like to teach. What they also saw was a teacher capitalizing on free time. The partner might have understood teachers' need to plan lessons and analyze data, but more than likely, teachers missed the opportunity to work *with* the community partner to deepen their understanding. Teachers must ensure that lessons focus on the curriculum and standards, a connection that partners may not see immediately. Second, spending time working *together* builds the relationship with the community partner, an essential foundation for advocating for innovations. The partner's presence alone doesn't make a partnership high quality. Quality comes from collaborating with the partner on curriculum.

WAITING FOR THE RIGHT TIME

A teacher once shared this story like this:

> *When I was thinking of having a baby, I wanted to wait for the "right" time. I thought I should be financially stable, have the right job, the perfect house. Well, my mom finally looked at me and said, "Natalie, there will never be a perfect time. If you want a baby, have the baby. Life will work out. It always does."*

Conditions do not need to be perfect before an educator begins CBL. Districts' financial picture will never be certain. The timing of new mandates is unpredictable. Curriculum alignment is a constant work in progress. These educational needs have to be tended to, but they should not stop innovation. When a teacher is excited about the idea, a unit has potential, or a partner is intrigued, the time is right. Remember that CBL can start small with those who are ready.

TOXIC LEADERS

Many schools and communities have toxic leaders, people who may appear to be supportive and say the right things, but whose interests are selfish. Liz Wiseman (Wiseman & McKeown, 2010) divides people into two types in her book *Multipliers: How the Best Leaders Make Everyone Smarter*: multipliers and diminishers. According to Wiseman, multipliers bring out the best in others and find personal success in the success of those they lead. Diminishers, she says, squelch talent and creative thinking, make decisions in isolation, seize control, and always seem to have (and share) the answers.

Any diminishers involved in CBL will almost certainly doom it to failure. District leaders can and should develop improvement plans, and possibly exit plans, for diminishers. If a partner exhibits toxic behaviors, then the partnership should be limited. Keep the lines of communication open and find a way for that partner to contribute; however, if the partner's toxicity will negatively affect learning or relationships, the boundaries for that partnership need to be tight.

A school board member named Ken, who also was a financial advisor, had a troubled history on the board. Ken was conservative, vocal, and seldom supported public education. He frequently berated other board members and publicly admonished them when they did not have full understanding of a financial issue. Ken's diminishing behaviors created an environment in which other board members were afraid to ask questions or offer opinions. They sat quietly while Ken made his point, and then the group voted. Most votes on financial issues were 6–1. When Ken learned about CBL, he asked to partner with the district. The superintendent had a choice. She could discourage Ken's interest, or she could find a teacher to work with him. She asked herself questions like, "Does the district have financial classes that could benefit from a partnership with a financial adviser? Can Ken be trusted to keep his political views in check and work with a teacher to present a nonpartisan financial CBL experience for children? After publicly criticizing teachers at board meetings, are the chances good for a successful educator-partner relationship?" In considering the latter questions, the superintendent was cautious. She feared the experience could become a catalyst for a personal agenda and walked away.

FACING DOWN DETRACTORS

Michael Fullan (2001) describes detractors as a critical element of the change process because detractors allow us to refine our thinking and remove our blinders. Negative attacks are learning opportunities. Remember the science teacher from the Communities School example who quizzed a student to find out if she had memorized the tree name? The concept behind the CBL experience is to increase community advocacy while providing students with relevant learning. It emphasizes critical thinking, collaboration, and academic benchmarks. For whatever reason, the school's science department did not like CBL. The team used the negative attack as an impetus to improve.

In *Leading in a Culture of Change*, Michael Fullan (2001) encourages educators to "redefine resistance as a potential positive force" (p. 5). Innovations are opportunities to educate those who do not understand the innovation or the motivations behind its implementation. Rather than allowing critics to stop progress, use their comments to improve the innovation.

GOOD TO GREAT

A superintendent from Minnesota expressed that his district had no need to implement CBL. "Everything is good in that area," he told the board. "We really don't have to work on school-community relations because the community is supportive." No one in the community was griping about taxes. There were no private schools to compete with for funds. Test scores were good, and no one was complaining about achievement. Collins states, "Good is the enemy of great" (Collins, 2001a, p. 1). Instruction may have been fine in this district, but teachers were not maximizing the possibilities. When things seem to be working, the temptation is to settle into a comfort zone instead of pushing for greatness. CBL would have required a relatively small shift in thinking in this district.

In fact, according to Pietersen (2002), "The best time to change . . . is when [an organization is] successful, but that's also the time when resistance to change is at its highest." Change would have required hard work, intentionally building trust, and allocating resources, but for the time was right for the district to preserve community relations. Homeostasis is delicate. By not tending to an area that seems satisfactory, educators will not reach greatness and may eventually find themselves in a state of decline.

EXISTING STRUCTURES

Education has a history of doing things a certain way, and deviating from that pattern can be a challenge. CBL requires change in two structural areas: curriculum and postsecondary preparation. Those planning CBL can stay within the current curriculum or create a new curriculum, which may seem simpler at first but requires an array of permissions. Curricular exceptions often need state and local approval. Even with approvals, writing a new curriculum is a *lot* of work. A more efficient solution is to use a project-based learning approach, which lends itself well to integrating curricula. Rather than focusing on changing the curriculum, educators focus on changing how they deliver and assess the curriculum. By keeping to the existing curriculum, teachers don't need formal permission for changes. The key is to find instructional methods that engage students. Continuing the same standards but changing the way they are learned allows teachers to individualize the curriculum without completely recreating it.

Changing delivery also may be complicated. The team in the CBL school in Chapter 4 had to work closely with school guidance department staff to ensure that students' credits for the program were reflected on their transcripts for college admissions. The CBL school found a way around this change, and ultimately institutions of higher learning understood and accepted the learning experiences on their own merits. Teachers need to work with post-secondary institutions to help them understand the value of experiential learning, how students build community connections and refine 21st century skills, so that admissions officials view CBL on a transcript as a sign a student is well prepared for advanced work.

WANTS OVER NEEDS

Years ago, a cleaning woman in a television commercial professed, "I don't do windows." Some viewers might have thought, "She is a cleaning woman. Why wouldn't she do windows?" The subtext of this commercial is that although the woman did not *want* to do windows, her job required it.

Discerning wants and needs is crucial to success in education today. Many teachers believe they are doing a good job and don't feel the need to change or involve the community—that community relations is not part of their job. Educators should ask themselves

- How has heightened public scrutiny and criticism of public education affected my school or district, and my practice?
- How is the current political climate affecting wages? Are education salaries stagnant? What role can I play in addressing this issue?
- How are we addressing increasing class sizes and reduced budgets for supplies?

Educators can develop the broader community's understanding and appreciation of educators' role and work. CBL offers that connection in a positive, productive, engaging learning experience for students. CBL may just be "cleaning the windows."

Sometimes preK–18 outcomes inhibit progress because they are misaligned. Some institutions of higher learning value the higher level thinking at the heart of the Common Core. Others do not. When an institution asks for community involvement and higher-order thinking skills from students, engaging in CBL is easier. But when an institution has a rigid, traditional approach to learning, implementing CBL is harder. In the latter cases, having conversations about the changing expectations in K–12 education is a good starting point. Another beginning point is to show them their needs by demonstrating how much better prepared students are when they enter the institution technologically capable, prepared to problem-solve, communicate, collaborate, and able to make evidence-based decisions.

Finally, educators should consider what the community wants and what it needs. School districts often perceive that the community wants high-quality instruction at a low cost. What the community needs is a collaborative relationship with schools in order to progress toward common goals. Society needs students who are prepared to improve communities through active contributions as an engaged and skilled citizen. It is easy to lose sight of this goal. Discussions turn quickly toward budgets and away from learning. An "us versus them" mentality emerges. Working *together* on outcomes makes it harder to be distracted from the goal.

Educators have the power to create and sustain change. Perceived barriers can get in the way, or we can blast through them to get to the right work. Decide on a strategy, such as CBL, and make the choice.

Questions for Reflection

1. Which barriers to CBL concern us most? How might they be addressed?
2. What barriers might be easier to overcome?
3. Where might we be impeding our own progress toward CBL?

CHAPTER 9

Starting Community– Based Learning— Today

MAIN IDEA

Every stakeholder has the ability to foster community-based learning. By taking individual steps toward implementing community-based learning, educators can affect systemic organizational change.

George Raveling was a young man in 1963 when he heard about a march in Washington, D.C., where Dr. Martin Luther King, Jr. would speak. Raveling had no plans to go. Not long before the march, a friend's father suggested that Raveling should attend because it was going to be a momentous event and, at the last minute, he did.

At the march, someone asked Raveling to volunteer. He agreed and was assigned security duty near center stage. That day, King delivered delivered his *I Have a Dream* speech. In a brief moment where the civil rights leader left the podium and passed Raveling, Raveling impetuously asked King for a copy of the speech. King gave it to the young man before being whisked away.

Fifty years later, the speech is framed in George Raveling's safety deposit box at a bank. What began as a casual suggestion to a young man resulted in him possessing one of the most famous documents in history. As improbable as the request might have seemed, George Raveling leaned in to the possibilities and found himself in a far better place than when he began (Harris & Gerard, 2013).

Every serendipitous event begins with a single step toward action. Once you understand the concept of community-based learning (CBL) and understand its framework, you likely see where possibilities exist in your own settings. Like all new ideas, you are probably thinking, "What do I do with this new information?" The answer is to "lean in" to CBL and see where the possibilities lead.

FOR TEACHERS

Consider your curriculum. Teachers ensure fidelity to the curriculum and control what is taught and how it is taught. Control of the curriculum is a responsibility—and an opportunity. To explore CBL, review the curriculum. Consider what students are expected to know and be able to do, and then ask how those concepts connect to the real world. Reflect on why standards and benchmarks are important for students and how to help them see the importance. Identify learning goal(s) and think about who in the community might have expertise in those areas. You do not need to identify an individual, just the role of the person you are looking for. For example, are you an art teacher trying to help students understand career possibilities? Consider museum curators, tattoo artists, pottery makers, stained glass window makers, landscape designers, interior decorators. Find connections to the learning goal, and then work on finding the people.

Once you have identified curricular connections, find someone who may help connect to those community partners. That person may be you if you know a lot of people in the community.

If you don't, find others in the district who are heavily embedded in community life, who seem to know everyone. When you find that highly connected individual, ask to brainstorm. For example, you might explain, "We are working on using math skills to balance a bank account. Do you know an accountant or banker who might be willing to work with us? Do you know which other people are in roles related to the topic?" It is as simple as that. Often a phone call is all that is needed to make a connection and begin a partnership, and you can be planning a lesson or unit within days.

FOR PRINCIPALS

Reflect on your staff. Which teachers are eager for a next step, a challenge? Some teachers are curriculum rocks stars. Others are stellar relationship builders. Still others are magnificent teachers, but need a change. Sometimes teachers approach their principal with an idea if they are familiar with CBL. If teachers do not approach you, you can suggest the idea to them and ask them to think about how it might work. If you educate your collective staff about CBL, consider which individuals among the whole group have their interest piqued.

If you are developing your school improvement goal, consider incorporating community partnerships into the achievement or teacher evaluation goals. The Interstate Teacher Assessment and Support Consortium (InTASC) standards (Council of Chief State School Officers, 2011) for teaching closely align with most evaluation frameworks for high-quality teaching practices. CBL can support teachers in working toward mastery of these and other standards. Improving instructional techniques, understanding how students learn, connecting to the community, and honing leadership skills are all critically important for teacher success. The CBL design can facilitate growth in each of these areas. You don't need to require CBL, but you *can* set broad parameters that the CBL strategy can meet. Parameters might include

- Increasing curricular partnerships within the community
- Researching and using instructional techniques that help students make meaning of content
- Improving student engagement

Principals can get CBL started through an individual conversation or global goal setting—or perhaps both. The choice is yours.

FOR SUPERINTENDENTS

Assess your community. Whether through surveys, in conversations with community members, or by reviewing media sources, ask yourself: How connected are you? How urgent is the need to develop community goals, a community agenda? What is the level of support from the community to the school? From the school to the community? If there are concerns about how well the district's message is being interpreted and understood, it is time as superintendent to make it a priority to build community engagement. CBL is one systemic strategy that can allow all staff to work on this goal while simultaneously teaching the curriculum and engaging students.

Include CBL within the established areas of focus for the district. Whether through formal goal setting, school improvement planning, or principal coaching, set clear expectations for implementing CBL and support the practice through education, permission, and accountability.

Before CBL can begin, the staff and the board of education need to know what it is. You may research the practice and communicate it, or the board or educators may get involved in a study of the concept. Whichever approach you take, helping others understand CBL is the precursor to action.

Once people understand CBL and its potential benefits, district leaders need to give permission for staff to engage in any level of CBL. Those adopting a new practice often fear doing something wrong. When people worry about doing something "right," they may be deterred from doing the "right" thing. Remind educators that attempting new strategies is valued, and take feedback to adjust the strategy to better meet student needs. Supporting calculated risk-taking is connected to accountability.

Attaining a goal requires communicating the necessary components, developing procedures to ensure those components are met, and then stepping away to let people work. This means allowing educators to explore potential partnerships and align unit benchmarks (although a district administrator might approve the CBL plan to ensure fidelity to the practice and curriculum before a staff member contacts a prospective partner). You might require that staff present assessment results or other indicators of success to the board of education. The superintendent sets the direction and keeps people accountable but allows them to make CBL happen.

FOR BOARDS OF EDUCATION

Boards of Education, which develop the policies and approve program resources, can have the most influence in implementating CBL. Board members set the tone by honoring innovation. The board might approve a philosophical statement about the importance of innovation, create financial incentives set up formal recognitions of desired practices, or create districtwide goals for a number of classroom or school partnerships within the community. Board support could include funding positions such as innovation coaches, a CBL coordinator, and community partnership liaisons. Boards members' support (or lack of support) helps create the district's focus and determines whether innovation is possible. If CBL is important to your district, actively work to develop successful and sustained CBL practices.

FOR EVERYONE

CBL is a new concept in K–12 education. Educators have just begun to think about ways to maximize community partnerships and how to develop community agendas to benefit schools and the community. Pockets of innovation that look like CBL or smaller scale CBL projects exist throughout education. In order for the practice to become more refined, educators need to learn the potential scope of the practice.

No matter what your role, now that you know about CBL, you are equipped to promote the idea, engage in it, and help others become familiar with it. Word of mouth is the best way to promote CBL and bring communities and schools closer to reawaken the mission of public schools.

By putting the pieces together to create CBL experiences, you can transform the academic and community aspects of your system. CBL allows maximum curricular and community relations impact with the mastery of a single strategy.

Questions for Reflection

1. In my role, what is one thing I can do to further CBL?
2. With whom do I have influence? How can I use that influence to promote CBL?
3. What action step will I take tomorrow to facilitate a closer connection between my community and the curriculum?

Appendix

Sample Community–Based Learning Unit

Neighborhood Study Unit

$\mathcal{T}$he purpose of this project is to develop a better understanding of neighborhoods and the quality of life within them. The information gained from these activities will then be used to construct a report about neighborhoods, including recommendations for addressing issues that we identify. We hope that participants will not only learn more about themselves and their community, but they will also be empowered to take action to improve it.

Project time frame: three weeks

STANDARDS

Literacy

W.1 Write arguments to support claims in an analysis of substantive topics using valid reasoning and relevant and sufficient evidence.

W.2 Write informative/explanatory texts to examine and convey complex ideas, concepts, and information.

W.4 Produce clear and coherent writing in which the development, organization, and style are appropriate.

SL.4 Present information, findings, and supportive evidence clearly, concisely, and logically such that listeners can follow.

SL.5 Make strategic use of digital media.

L.6 Accurately use general academic and domain-specific words and phrases sufficient for writing.

Social Studies

WCU9 A1.1/USH 10A1.1 Know the location of political and physical features.

WCU9 A1.3/USH 10 A1.2 Understand the interaction between the environment and humans.

WCU9 E1.2 Understand the forces that shape individuals, groups, and institutions.

USH 10E1.1 Understand how individual and group perspectives are shaped by shared experiences.

Science

Understand biological classification through use of dichotomous keys.

Leadership

LED.12.A.1.1 Understand how trust affects interpersonal relationships.

LED.12.A.1.5 Participate actively in team activities.

LED.12.B.2.1 Understand the steps involved in setting up a successful project.

LED.12.B.2.3 Demonstrate the ability to evaluate and alter the plan before, during, or after the project.

LED.12.C.1.1 Understand the role of communication in leadership.

LED.12.C.1.2 Adapt communication style to situation and audience.

LED.12.C.1.3 Communicate in a variety of public settings.

LED.12.C.3.1 Use effective speaking techniques.

LED.12.C.3.2 Understand how tone impacts verbal communication.

LED.12.C.4.1 Understand the importance of active listening.

LED.12.C.6.1 Understand nonverbal forms of communication.

UNINTENTIONAL BENCHMARKS

CCH.12.K.3.3 Know interviewing skills for a job.

CCG.12.K.4.1 Understand the importance of networking techniques for professional growth.

ART.12.E.1.2 Communicate an idea using photos, graphic designs, or multi-media.

Activities

*Step 1: *3 2 1 Bridge.* When thinking about your neighborhood what are 3 Words, 2 Questions, 1 Metaphor/Simile? *(Alone in advisory: 15–20 min).*
Step 2: Partner, Paul V.A Sociology Professor at university (LRC) (8:00–8:25).
Step 3: Pretest 6 Questions (*Free Flow Time—Blog in computer lab or own device 15 min).*
Step 4: *Draw a map of your neighborhood.* Simply take a pen and a sheet of paper (the larger, the better) and draw (*Open time: 30 min).*

- The boundaries, clearly marking the northern, southern, eastern, and western boundaries (streets or physical features) of the area that you consider to be your neighborhood.
- Then, draw in the following details within those boundaries, as they apply to you and your neighborhood:
  - *Major streets*
  - *Landmarks (natural features, historical buildings, etc., that are well-known to people in this area)*
  - *Parks*
  - *Stores, restaurants, bars, etc.*
  - *Public facilities (schools, government buildings)*

- o *Houses of worship*
- o *Other gathering places*
- o *The place where you currently live*
- o *The place where you currently work (if it is within the boundaries)*
- o *Places where people you know on a first-name basis live*
- o *Anything else of importance in your neighborhood*

*When drawing your map, we don't expect you to be a cartographer. However, keep map scale, direction, distance, and legend in mind. Submit a draft by the end of Wednesday, September 12th.
Step 4B: Reflect on the process of drawing your mental map.

Step 5: *Use Google Maps.* Use this Google Maps on smartphones or in lab to refine your mental map of your neighborhood.
Step 6: Self & Peer Assessment of Maps (9 or 10 SL.2)
Step 7: Evernote
Step 8: Blog: State Assembly Representative or Analyzing the Effectiveness of Their Self- and Peer Assessment (9 or 10) *(at home)*
Step 9: *Guest Speakers—Realtor, Appraiser.* The three speakers will address what features in your neighborhood add value and devalue your neighborhood. Each speaker will speak with 25 students. *(3 classrooms—40 min)*
Step 10: *Handout Neighborhood Courtesy/Informational Sheet.* This handout will notify neighbors of the students of the activity being conducted in their neighborhood. *(computer lab—2 hr)*

Step 11: *Guest Speakers—Christine H (Art Teacher), Andy R (Camera business), Dee M. (Photography business).* The guest speakers will address what to consider to take a good picture. *(3 classrooms—30 min)*
Step 12: *Take photographs around your neighborhood* (as defined by your map) that fall into the following categories:

1. Places or things that you value (for social, economic, cultural, ecological, and/or recreational reasons)

2. Places or things that you believe have changed in recent years

3. Places or things that you feel should be preserved and/or fixed up/modified

4. When you are thinking about your neighborhood, places/landmarks that come to mind

5. People who you feel represent who lives in your neighborhood

6. Your most important neighborhood hangout (a place that is not home, not work)

7. One image that best captures the overall essence of the neighborhood (what it's all about)

Step 13: Blog: What places or things add value or devalue (for social, economic, cultural, ecological, and/or recreational reasons) your neighborhood?

Please take at least one (1) photo in each category, but not more than fifteen (15) total photos, ideally with your own digital camera; let us know if you need a camera, and we will provide one and reimburse you for the cost of developing hard copies, if applicable. If possible, take some time to carefully think about which places/things/landmarks/people offer the best fit for you with the above photo categories, and have fun with it!

Step 14: *Exit Interview With Teachers.* Each student will interview with a teacher to summatively assess their knowledge and skills gained throughout the project. (Language & SL1)

Step 15: *Interview:* Once you have completed the first two steps, please contact us to schedule an interview, which will use your map and photos as the basis for a discussion about your neighborhood and life in Oshkosh. We will view the map/photos together and ask you a series of questions related to our research topic.

Step 16: *Culminating Activity:*

1. Choose an image that best captures the overall essence of the neighborhood. Include a summary.

2. Rationalize why they chose the image. Significance, adds value, or devalues your neighborhood.

   • Choose an image that you feel should be preserved and/or fixed/modified.

Assessments

Mental Map

Photo and Summarization

Technology used

Google Maps

Scan in Mental Maps

Camera

Adobe Photoshop

Community-based learning pillar: Place-based education partners

Paul VA, PhD, University Sociology Department

Steve P, Realtor

Chuck W, Realtor

Christina H, Art teacher

Andy R, Camera business

Dee M, Photography business

Source: Julie Dumke, Richard Leib, Oliver Schinkten, and Brad Weber, Oshkosh Area School District, 2013. Used with permission.

References

Aguilar, E. (2008, September 23). Why integrate: A case for collating the curriculum [Online forum comment]. Retrieved from http://www.edutopia.org/integrated-authentic

Aikin, W. (n.d.) *The story of the eight-year study.* New York, NY: Harper and Brothers. Retrieved from http://www.archive.org/stream/storyoftheeighty009637mbp/storyoftheeighty009637mbp_djvu.txt

Ainsworth, L., & Viegut, D. (2006). *Common formative assessments: How to connect standards-based instruction and assessment.* Thousand Oaks, CA: Corwin.

ASCD. (2012). *The whole child.* Retrieved from http://www.wholechildeducation.org/about

Bartsch, J., & Contributing Teachers. (2001). *Community lessons: Promising curriculum practices.* Malden, MA: Massachusetts Department of Education. Retrieved from http://www.doe.mass.edu/csl/comlesson.pdf

Baughman, O. (2011). *Coffee to compost: Lessons from the front lines.* Retrieved from https://docs.google.com/document/d/10aVawR_fIuOpDTfg2bXTlUYBLwTATPGFj7Eh90XcBsE/edit

Beane, J. (1995). Curriculum integration and the disciplines of knowledge. *The Phi Delta Kappan, 76*(8), 616–622. Retrieved from http://www/jstor.org/stable/20405413

Bereiter, C., & Scardamalia, M. (1989). *Intentional learning as a goal of instruction.* Retrieved from http://ikit.org/fulltext/1989intentional.pdf

Big Thought. (n.d.). *Who we are.* Retrieved from www.bigthought.org/WhoWeAre

Blanchard, K., & Johnson, S. (2003). *The one-minute manager.* New York, NY: William Morrow.

Blake-Davis, L. [Principal] (2012, February). *Becket Washington school: The voice of the future.* Retrieved from http://www.edline .net/files/_sCKxV_/110c6cfb3e3789483745a49013852 ec4/4–23_INNOVATION_PLAN.pdf

Bransom, J., Denson, K., Hoitsma, L., & Pinto, M. (2010). *Creative learning: People and pathways.* Dallas, TX: Thriving Minds. Retrieved from http://www.creatingquality.org/Portals/1/DN NArticleFiles/634487500440325228Creative%20Learn-ing%20People%20and%20Pathways.pdf

Brzovic, K., & Matz, S. (2009). Students advise Fortune 500 company: Designing a problem-based learning community. *Business Communication Quarterly, 72*(1), 21–34. doi: 10.1177/1080569908321439

Buck Institute for Education. (2013). *Project based learning for the 21st century.* Retrieved from http://www.bie.org/

Carini, R., Kuh, G., & Klein, S. (in press). Student engagement and student learning: Testing the linkages. *Research in Higher Education.* Retrieved from http://nsse.iub.edu/pdf/research_ papers/testing_linkages.pdf

Carlisle, K. (2011). Inspire: The quest for coherent curriculum through a performing arts-focused curriculum integration project. *Middle Grades Research Journal, 6*(4), 223–234.

Carpenter, T., Fennema, E., Peterson, P., Chiang, C., & Loef, M. (1989). Using knowledge of children's mathematics thinking in classroom teaching: An experimental study. *American Education Research, 26*(4), 499–531.

Carvallo, A., & Paine, S. (2011, September). *Strategies for rescuing failing public schools: How leaders create a culture of success.* Retrieved from http://mcgraw-hillresearchfoundation.org/ wp-content/uploads/2011/09/Strategies-For-Rescuing-Failing-Public-Schools_whitepaper_Sept2011.pdf

Center for Ecoliteracy. (2013). *Teach: Place-based learning.* Retrieved from http://www.ecoliteracy.org/strategies/place-based-learning

Clarkson University. (2012). *Project-based learning partnership.* Retrieved from http://www.clarkson.edu/highschool/k12/

Cole, D. (1989). *The effects of a one-year staff development program on the achievement test scores of fourth grade students* (Doctoral dissertation). Available from ProQuest. (UMI No. 9232258)

Collins, J. (2001a). *Good to great* (1st ed.). New York, NY: Harper Collins.

Collins, J. (2001b, October). *Good to great. Fast company.* Retrieved from http://www.jimcollins.com/article_topics/articles/good-to-great.html

Collins, J. (2012). *Defining greatness.* Retrieved from http://www.jimcollins.com/media_topics/defining.html#audio=32

Common Core State Standards Initiative. (2013). *Mission statement.* Retrieved from http://www.corestandards.org/

Connick, W. (2013, July 17). *What is cold calling?* Retrieved from sales.about.com/od/glossaryofsalesterms/g/What-Is-Cold-Calling.htm

Cortez-Riggio, K. M. (2011). The green footprint project: How middle school students inspired their community and raised their self-worth. *English Journal, 100*(3), 39–43. Retrieved from http://gsep.pepperdine.edu/news-events/media-resources/clips/english-journal.pdf

Council of Chief State School Officers. (2011, April). *Interstate Teacher Assessment and Support Consortium (InTASC) model core teaching standards: A resource for state dialogue.* Washington, DC: Author.

D'Amelio, J. (Producer). (2011). Whistle stop [Television series episode]. In Lane, N. (Executive Producer), *CBS Sunday Morning.* New York, NY: CBS. Retrieved from http://www.cbsnews.com/video/watch/?id=7409106n

Danielson, C. (2013). *The Famework.* Princeton, NJ: The Danielson Group. Retrieved from danielsongroup.org

Danielson, C., & McGreal, T. L. (2000). *Teacher evaluation to enhance professional practice.* Alexandria, VA: ASCD.

Darling-Hammond, L. (2010). *The flat world and education: How America's commitment to equity will determine our future (multicultural education).* New York, NY: Teachers College Press.

David, J. (2008). What research says about project-based learning. *Educational Leadership, 65*(5), 80–82. Retrieved from http://www.ascd.org/publications/educational_leadership/feb08/v0165/num05/Project-Based_Learning.aspx

Dean, C., Hubbell, E., Pitler, H., & Stone, B.J. (2012). *Classroom instruction that works: Research-based strategies for increasing student achievement* (2nd ed.). Alexandria, VA: ASCD.

DelMonte, J. (2013, July). *High-quality professional development for teachers.* Retrieved from www.americanprogress.org

Dewey, J. (1938). *Logic: The theory of inquiry.* United States of America: Henry Holt and Company. Retrieved from

http://ia601606.us.archive.org/30/items/JohnDeweyLogic-
TheTheoryOfInquiry/[John_Dewey]_Logic_-_The_Theory_
of_Inquiry.pdf

Dickmann, M., & Stanford-Blair, N. (2009). *Mindful leadership:
A brain-based framework.* Thousand Oaks, CA: Corwin.

Diggs, T. (Performer). (2013, February 22). Kellogg's shares
breakfast with Hodge Elementary [Web Video]. Retrieved from
http://www.youtube.com/watch?v=1TghZ_9GZRw

Drake, S., & Burns, R. (2004). *Meeting standards through integrated
curriculum.* Alexandria, VA: ASCD.

Dudley, D. (Performer). (2010). *Drew Dudley: Everyday leadership.*
[Web Video]. Retrieved from http://www.ted.com/talks/drew_
dudley_everyday_leadership.html

Duffy, G. G., Roehler, L. R., Meloth, M. S., Vavrus, L. G., Book, C.,
Putnam, J., et al. (1986). The relationship between explicit
verbal explanations during reading skill instruction and student awareness and achievement: A study of reading teacher
effects. *Reading Research Quarterly, 21*(3), 237–252.

DuFour, R. (2007). In praise of top down leadership: What drives
your school improvement efforts—Evidence of best practice
or the pursuit of universal buy-in? *The School Administrator,
10*(64). Retrieved from http://aasa.org/SchoolAdministra-
torArticle.aspx?id=6498

DuFour, R. (2004). What is a professional learning community?
Educational Leadership, 61(8), 6–11.

Dweck, C. (2006). *Mindset: The new psychology of success.*
New York, NY: Random House.

Ellis, K. (Producer). (2007, October 03). Kids invest in funds—and
their own future [Web Video]. Retrieved from http://www
.edutopia.org/ariel-financial-literacy-math-stocks-video

Elmore, R. (2000). *Building a new structure for school leadership.*
Retrieved from http://www.politicalscience.uncc.edu/godwink/
PPOL8687/Wk10_March_22_Accountability/Elmore_
Building_a_New_Structure_for_School_Leadership.pdf

Epstein, J. (1995). School/family/community partnerships:
Caring for the children we share. *Phi Delta Kappan, 76*(9),
701–712. Retrieved from https://services.online.missouri
.edu/exec/data/courses2/coursegraphics/2226/L5-Epstein
.pdf

Flavell, J. (1979). Metacognition and cognitive monitoring:
A new era of cognitive-developmental inquiry. *American*

Psychologist, 34(10), 906–911. Retrieved from http://www4
.ncsu.edu/~jlnietfe/Metacog_Articles_files/Flavell (1979).pdf

Freeman, E. (2010). *Strategic management: A stakeholder approach.*
New York, NY: Cambridge University Press.

Fullan, M. (2001). *Leading in a culture of change.* San Francisco,
CA: Jossey-Bass.

Goldsmith, M., Greensberg, C. L., Robertson, A., & Hu-Chan, M.
(2003). *Global leadership: The next generation.* Upper Saddle
River, NJ: Prentice Hall.

Greater Beloit Works. (2012). *The Greater Beloit Economic
Development Corporation annual report.* Retrieved from http://
www.greaterbeloitworks.com/Portals/0/GBEDCAnnual
Report2012.pdf

Greater Beloit Economic Development Corporation. (2012,
March 27). *Support of the school district of Beloit referendum.*
Retrieved from http://www.slideshare.net/beloitworks/support-
of-the-school-district-of-beloit-referendum

Guskey, T. (2002). Does it make a difference? Evaluating professional development. *Educational Leadership, 59*(6), 45–51.

Hargreaves, A., & Fullan, M. G. (1992). *Understanding teacher
development.* New York, NY: Teachers College Press.

Harris, T. A. (Writer), & Gerard, N. (Director). (2013, September
16). Guardian of history: MLK's "I have a dream speech" lives
on [Television Series Episode]. In A. Patrick (Producer), CBS
Sunday Morning. New York, NY: CBS Interactive Inc.

Hartzler, D. (2000, May). *A meta-analysis of studies conducted on
integrated curriculum programs and their effects on student
achievement.* Bloomington, IN: Indiana University.

Hassel, E., U.S. Department of Education, Office of Educational
Research. (1999). *Professional development: Learning from
the best.* Naperville, IL: North Central Regional Educational
Laboratory.

Hattie, J. (2009). *Visible learning: A synthesis of over 800 meta-
analyses relating to achievement.* New York, NY: Routledge.

Henderson, A., & Mapp, K. U.S. Department of Education,
Education Sciences. (2002). *A new wave of evidence: The impact
of school, family, and community connections on student achievement.* Austin, TX: SEDL. Retrieved from http://www.sedl.org/
connections/resources/evidence.pdf

Hilf, A. (2013, June 6). Local business owner helping keep art alive in
Naches Valley. *KDNU.* Retrieved from http://kndu.membercenter

.worldnow.com/story/22526657/local-business-owner-helping-keep-art-alive-in-naches-valley

International Center for Leadership in Education. (n.d.). *Rigor/relevance framework*. Retrieved from http://www.leadered.com/pdf/R&Rframework.pdf

Jackson, D. (2001). *Twin tales: The magic and mystery of multiple births*. New York, NY: Warner Books.

Jennings, N. R., & Mamdani, E. H. (1992). Using joint responsibility to coordinate collaborative problem solving in dynamic environments. In the *10th National Conference on Artificial Intelligence (AAAI-92)*. San Jose, CA.

Kennerly, M., & Neely, A. (2003). Measuring performance in a changing business environment. *International Journal of Operations & Production Management, 23*(2). Retrieved from https://www.som.cranfield.ac.uk/som/dinamic-content/research/cbp/IJOPM_v23_n2.pdf

Kirton, M. (1976). Adaptors and innovators: A description and measure. *Journal of Applied Psychology, 61*(5), 622–629.

Klein, J. (2011, April 26). *The failure of American schools*. Retrieved from http://www.theatlantic.com/magazine/archive/2011/06/the-failure-of-american-schools/308497/

Kolb, D. (1984). *Experiential learning: Experience as the source of learning and development*. Upper Saddle River, NJ: Prentice Hall.

Lawrimore, B. (2011). *Key success factors*. Retrieved from http://totalsuccesscenter.com/business-success/key-success-factors/

Layton, L. (2013, December 2). *U.S. students lag around average on international science, math and reading test*. Retrieved from http://www.washingtonpost.com/local/education/us-students-lag-around-average-on-international-science-math-and-reading-test/2013/12/02/2e510f26–5b92–11e3-a49b-90a0e156254b_story.html

Lewin, K. (1947). Frontiers in group dynamics: Concept, method and reality in social science; Social equilibria and social change. *Human Relations, 1*(5), 5–40. doi: 10:1177001872674700100103

Management Pocketbooks. (2010, September 7). *Social networks—A short early history*. Retrieved from http://managementpocketbooks.wordpress.com/tag/sociogram/

Mann, D. (2010). *Creating a lean culture: Tools to sustain lean conversations*. (2nd ed.). New York, NY: Productivity Press Taylor & Francis Group.

Marek, E. A., & Methven, S. B. (1991). Effects of the learning cycle upon student and classroom teacher performance. *Journal of Research in Science Teaching, 28*(1), 41–53.

Marzano, R. (2003). *What works in schools.* Alexandria, VA: ASCD.

Marzano, R. (1992). *A different kind of classroom: Teaching with dimensions of learning.* Alexandria, VA: ASCD.

Mathews, D. (1996). *Is there a public for public schools?* Dayton, OH: Charles F. Kettering Foundation.

Maxwell, J. A. (2005). *Qualitative research design: An interactive approach* (2nd ed.).Thousand Oaks, CA: Sage.

Mayer-Mihalski, N., & DeLuca, M. (2009, May). *Effective education leading to behavior change.* Retrieved from http://www.paragonrx .com/experience/white-papers/effective-education-leading-to-behavior-change

McCaffrey, S. (2013, April 11). School board candidate Kanninen wants more responsiveness to parents, public. *Sun Gazette.* Retrieved from http://www.sungazette.net/arlington/ education/school-board-candidate-kanninen-wants-more-responsiveness-to-parents-public/article_526de5d8-a29b-11e2–9691–001a4bcf887a.html

McCutchen, D., Abbott, R. D., Green, L. B., Beretvas, S. N., Cox, S., Potter, N. S., et al. (2002). Beginning literacy: Links among teacher knowledge, teacher practice, and student learning. *Journal of Learning Disabilities, 35*(1), 69–86.

McGill-Franzen, A., Allington, R. L., Yokoi, L., & Brooks, G. (1999). Putting books in the classroom seems necessary but not sufficient. *Journal of Educational Research, 93*(2), 67–74.

McNulty, R. (2011, September). *Transitional leadership skills for the transformation of public education in Wisconsin.* Presentation delivered at Wisconsin School Leadership Center Initial Keynote, Madison, WI.

Melaville, A., Jacobson, R., & Blank, M. J. (2011). *Scaling up school and community partnerships: The community schools strategy.* Washington, DC: Coalition for Community Schools, Institute for Educational Leadership.

Merrow, J. (Performer). (2013, April 3). *PBS NewsHour: School district uses project based learning over testing.* [Web Video]. Retrieved from http://video.pbs.org/video/2364990349/

Mertens, B., Cherry, R., & Taylor, C. (2010, October 1). [Radio broadcast]. Madison, WI: The Idea Network of Wisconsin Public Radio.

Miller, L., & Parsons, C. (2010). *Dare: Teaching students good decision-making skills to help them lead safe and healthy lives.* Retrieved from www.dare.org

Mind Tools. (1999). *Mission statements and vision statements.* Retrieved from www.mindtools.com/pages/article/newLDR_90.htm

Moos, J. (Performer). (2013, March 7). *Man pushes his girlfriend off a cliff* [Web Video]. Retrieved from http://www.youtube.com/watch?v=GPVzfjXxF28

Moreno, J. L. (1953). *Who shall survive? Foundations of sociometry, group psychotherapy, and sociodrama.* Beacon, NY: Beacon House.

National Commission on Teaching and America's Future. (2013). *About NCTAF.* Retrieved from http://nctaf.org/about-nctaf/

National Service Learning Clearinghouse. (2013). *What is service learning?* Retrieved from http://www.servicelearning.org/what-is-service-learning

Neal, D., Wood, W., & Drolet, A. (2013). How do people adhere to goals when willpower is low? The profits (and pitfalls) of strong habits. *Journal of Personality and Social Psychology, 104*(6), 959–975.

Net Industries. (2013). *Eight-year study—Purpose, method, results.* Retrieved from http://education.stateuniversity.com/pages/1947/Eight-Year-Study.html

Newmann, F., & Wehlage, G. (1995, October 30). *Successful school restructuring: A report to the public and educators.* Retrieved from http://www.wcer.wisc.edu/archive/cors/Successful_School_Restruct.html

Nistler, P. (Performer). (2009, May 20). Ariens Technology and Engineering Education Center Blueprint: Designing Wisconsin's Future [Print Photo]. Retrieved from http://www.youtube.com/watch?v=FCF3BZsCdsU

No Child Left Behind Title IX, Part A, Sections 9101 (2001).

Orentlicher, D. (Performer). (April 5, 2013). Joy Cardin [Radio series episode]. In Mertens, B. (Executive Producer), *Ideas Network.* Madison, WI: Wisconsin Public Radio. Retrieved from http://wpr.org/cardin/

Paine, S., & McCann, R., & U.S. Department of Education. (2009). *Engaging stakeholders: Including parents and the community to sustain improved reading outcomes.* Retrieved from RMC Research Corporation website: http://www2.ed.gov/programs/readingfirst/support/stakeholderlores.pdf

Partnership for 21st Century Skills. (2011). *Framework for 21st century learning.* Retrieved from http://www.p21.Org/overview

Patrick, A. (Producer). (2013, August 18). Guardian of history: MLK's "I have a dream speech" lives on. [Print Photo]. Retrieved from http://www.cbsnews.com/8301–3445_162–57596990/guardian-of-history-mlks-i-have-a-dream-speech-lives-on/

Piaget, J. (1954). *The construction of reality in the child.* New York, NY: Basic Books. Retrieved from http://books.google.com/books?hl=en&lr=&id=hK37xrpqdIkC&oi=fnd&pg=PA3&dq=The_construction_of_reality_in_the_child&ots=yf6GoSBBbW&sig=InMlXALTiYxr1FfKfrk202qzf-g

Pieterson, W. (2002, September/October). The Mark Twain dilemma: The theory and practice of change leadership. *Journal of Business Strategy, 23*(5), 32–37. Retrieved from http://williepietersen.com/pdf/Mark_Twain_Dilemma.pdf

Post Primary Teachers' Association. (2013). *Research report: Professional learning and development.* Retrieved from www.ppta.org.nz

Queensland Government. (2013). *From shared learning goal to community engagement—Woodridge State High School.* Department of Education, Training and Employment. Retrieved from https://classroomconnections.eq.edu.au/topics/Pages/2013/issue-8/woodridge-shs.aspx

Richards, H., Brown, A., & Forde, T. (2006). *Addressing diversity in schools: Culturally responsive pedagogy.* National Center for Culturally Responsive Education Systems. Retrieved from http://www.nccrest.org/Briefs/Diversity_Brief.pdf

Sandhya, N. (2009, April 22). Daily lesson plan: An arm and a leg. *The New York Times.* Retrieved from http://www.nytimes.com/learning/teachers/lessons/20090422wednesday.html

Sanders, M. (2006). *Building school-community partnerships.* Thousand Oaks, CA: Corwin.

Saxe, G. B., Gearhart, M., & Nasir, N. S. (2001). Enhancing students' understanding of mathematics: A study of three contrasting approaches to professional support. *Journal of Mathematics Teacher Education, 4*(1), 55–79.

Schlechty, P. (2011). *Engaging students: The next level of working on the work.* San Francisco, CA: Jossey-Bass.

Schneider, E., & Hollengzer, L. (2006). *The principal's guide to managing communications.* Thousand Oaks, CA: Corwin.

School District of Beloit. (2012). *Referendum 2012.* Retrieved from http://www.sdb.k12.wi.us/relations/referendum_2012.htm

Senge, P. (1990). *The fifth discipline: The art and practice of a learning organization.* New York, NY: Doubleday.

Senge, P. (2011). *Summary: The fifth discipline.* Kennett Square, PA: Soundview Executive Book Summaries. Retrieved from www .summary.com

Shaw, R. B. (1997). *Trust in the balance, building successful organizations on results, integrity, and concern.* San Francisco, CA: Jossey-Bass.

Sheehy, K. (2013, June 19). STEM high schools built on more than science and math. *U.S. News and World Report.* Retrieved from http://www.usnews.com/education/blogs/high-school-notes/2013/06/19/stem-high-schools-built-on-more-than-science-and-math

Sheppard, B., & Brown, J. (2009). Developing and implementing a shared vision of teaching and learning at the district level. *ISEA, 37*(2), 41–59.

Sinek, S. (Performer). (2009, September). Simon Sinek: How great leaders inspire action [Web Video]. Retrieved from www.ted.com/talks/simon_sinek_how_great_leaders_inspire_action.html

Sinek, S. (2009). *Start with why: How great leaders inspire everyone to take action.* New York, NY: Penguin Books.

Sloan, H. (1993). *Direct instruction to fourth and fifth grade classrooms.* (Doctoral dissertation). Available from ProQuest. (UMI No. 9334424)

Smith, J. (2013, July 1). Two Berkshire schools, part of state's innovation schools pilot program, reflect on past year. *The Berkshire Eagle News.* Retrieved from http://www.berkshireeagle .com/news/ci_23573748/two-berkshire-schools-part-states-innovation-schools-pilot

Sobel, D. (2005). *Place-based education: Connecting classrooms & communities.* Great Barrington, MA: The Orion Society.

Spillane, J., Halverson, R., & Diamond, J. (2001). Investigating school leadership practice: A distributed practice. *Educational Researcher, 30*(3), 23–28. Retrieved from http://olms.noinc .com/olms/data/resource/7712/Distributed Leadership.pdf

Stein, J. (2010). Choice and a public education: Core civic challenge. *Education Canada, 42*(4), 4–7. Retrieved from www .cea-ace.ca

Stein Rogan & Partners. (2008). *The "digital disconnect" disconnected communities are impeding district, school and student success.* Stein-Rogan Partners, LLC. Retrieved from http://digitaldisconnect.net/SWS_ResearchSummary.pdf

Strand, R. (2008). *The stakeholder dashboard.* Sheffield, UK: Greenleaf Publishing.

Tabor, B. (2013, March 7). Kellogg's promotes local school's effort with video. *Denton Record Chronicle.* Retrieved from http://www.dentonrc.com/local-news/local-news-headlines/20130307-kelloggs-promotes-local-schools-effort-with-video.ece

Texas Education Agency. (2013, February 1). *Texas 2012 NCLB report card.* Retrieved from http://ritter.tea.state.tx.us/cgi/sas/broker

The International High School. (2013). *Curriculum.* Retrieved from http://ihsnyc.org/

Tienken, C. (2003). *The effect of staff development in the use of scoring rubrics and reflective questioning strategies on fourth grade students' narrative writing performance.* Available from ProQuest. (UMI No. 3081032)

Timperley, H., & International Bureau of Education. (2008). *Teacher professional learning and development* (Educational Practices Series 18). Retrieved from International Academy of Education website: http://www.ibe.unesco.org

Uhlig, K. (2013, April 8). Reforms sweep up principals, too. *Wausau Daily Herald,* pp. 1–A.

U.S. Environmental Protection Agency. (2011). *Service learning: Learning by doing.* (3rd ed.). Washington, DC: Retrieved from http://nepis.epa.gov

Vars, G., & Beane, J. (2000). Integrative curriculum in a standards-based world. *Clearinghouse on Elementary and Early Childhood Education.* ERIC Digest, EDO-PS-00–6. Retrieved from http://ecap.crc.illinois.edu/eecearchive/digests/2000/vars00.pdf

Vars, G. (1991, October). Integrated curriculum in historical perspective. *Educational Leadership, 49*(2), 14–15.

Vollmer, J. (2010). *Schools cannot do it alone: Building public support for America's public schools.* Fairfield, IA: Enlightenment Press.

Vygotsky, L. (1978). *Mind in society: The development of higher psychological processes.* (14th ed.). United States: President and Fellows of Harvard College.

Wagner, T. (2010). *The global achievement gap: Why even our best schools don't teach the new survival skills our children need—and what we can do about it.* New York, NY: Basic Books.

Webb, N. (2002, March 28). *Depth-of-knowledge levels for four content areas.* Retrieved from http://www.providenceschools.org/media/55488/depth_of_knowledge_guide_for_all_subject_areas.pdf

Wiggins, G. P., & McTighe, J. (1998). *Understanding by design.* Alexandria, VA: ASCD.

Wiggins, G., & McTighe, J. (2011). *Understanding by design: Creating high quality units.* Alexandria, VA: ASCD.

Wiseman, L., & McKeown, G. (2010). *Multipliers: How the best leaders make everyone smarter.* New York: Harper Business.

Yan, C. (2003). *The Institute for Community Research.* Retrieved from http://www.incommunityresearch.org/news/ Saturday-night101Release.pdf

Yukl, G. (2006). *Leadership in organizations.* Upper Saddle River, NJ: Pearson Learning Solutions.

Young, T. W. (1990). *Public alternative education: Options and choice for today's schools.* New York, NY: Teachers College Press.

Index

Accountability, 54, 62, 98
  See also Assessments
Ambassadors, 89
Ariel Community Academy
    example, 90
Ariens Technology and Engineering
    Education Center example, 28
Assessments
  designing, 31–32, 33
  importance of, 42
  innovative data in, 101–102
  leveraging, 42–43, 44–45 (table), 47
  Neighborhood Study example, 120
  partnerships and, 67–70, 68
      (table), 69 (table), 70
  revising, 98–99
  South High School example,
      54–55, 58
Authentic pedagogy, 73–74
Automobile lesson, 93–94

Barriers to change
  cliff jumping example, 97–98
  detractors, 104
  existing structures, 105–106
  "good enough" mindset, 105
  lack of partnership
      relationship, 102
  large-scale tests, 100
  risk aversion, 100–102
  time issues, 98–100
  toxic leaders, 103–104
  waiting process, 103
  "wants over needs" focus, 106–107
  See also Change agents

Beane, James, 78, 79
Benchmarks, 27, 117
  logs, 67, 68 (table)
Black History lesson example, 37
Blank, M. J., 22
Blog activities, 119
Board of education involvement,
      58, 113
Boys and Girls Club example, 29
Burns, R., 78

California State University, Fullerton,
      12–13
Carlisle, Katie, 37
Case study
  beginnings, 49–52
  challenges, 53–55
  curriculum creation, 55–56
  exceeding expectations, 57–59
  progress, 52–53
  setbacks, 56–57
C2C (Coffee 2 Compost) program, 30
Celebrations, 34, 35, 41
Center for Occupational Research and
      Development (CORD), 79
Center on Organization and
      Restructuring of Schools, 73–74
Champions, 64–65
Change agents, 61–62, 89
  See also Barriers to change
Coffee 2 Compost (C2C) program, 30
Cold calls, 29, 32
Collaboration, 8, 21–22, 82
Collins, Jim, 63, 105
Common agendas, 21–22

Common Core Standards
  accountability, 98
  challenges, 79
  comparisons, 13, 14 (table)
  instructional change needed
      with, 12
  place-based learning and, 5–6
  tests as barriers, 100
Common vocabulary, 26–28
Communication, 7, 81
Communities
  changing definitions of, 18–19
  connections with, 3–4, 15–17,
      113–114
  developing, 80–81
  importance of, 15, 16–18, 89
  rubrics for, 45 (figure)
  student contributions to, 74
  "wants over needs" barrier,
      106–107
Community Lessons unit, 30–31
Connections, 16–17
  See also Communities
CORD (Center for Occupational
    Research and Development), 79
Core tenets of CBL, 92
Creating a Lean Culture (Mann), 40
Culminating activities, 119
Curriculum
  authentic pedagogy and, 73–74
  case study, 55–56
  experiential learning and, 2–3
  identifying goals, 30–31, 33
  integrating, 77–80, 110–111
  purposeful instruction and, 65–66
  relevant and experiential, 2–3
  South High School example,
      55–56
Customer service sessions, 81
Customization, 66–67

The Daily Lesson Plan units, 37
Dallas, Texas example, 68
Dashboards, 25–26, 40
David, Jane, 14
Dean, C., 15
Decision makers as targets, 29–30, 32

DelMonte, Jenny, 75–76
DeLuca, M., 101
Detractors, 104
Dewey, John, 12, 15
Dickmann, Michael, 14
Diminishers, 103–104
Distributive leadership, 89–91
Drake, S., 78
Drucker, Peter, 42
Dudley, Drew, 85–86

Early successes, 62–63
Educators
  evaluating, 100–101, 111
  rubrics for, 44 (figure)
  staff selection, 63–64
  teacher actions, 110–111
  work of, 1–2, 9
  See also Professional development
Elevator speeches, 36
Elmore, Richard, 89
Engagement of students, 2, 4–5,
      54–56, 58
Entry points, 28, 32
Evaluations of educators,
      100–101, 111
Existing structures as barriers,
      105–106
Experiential learning, 2–3,
      12–13, 106
Experimentation, 82
Experts, 82

The Fifth Discipline (Senge), 74
Flavell, J., 12
Framework of community-based
    learning
  assessing and improving, 42–47
  common vocabulary, 26–28
  implementation, 40–41, 92–95
  planning, 28–33
  vision setting, 22–26
  See also Partnerships;
      Sustainability plans
Franklin Springs example, 32–33,
      40–41, 62
Fullan, Michael, 104

GBEDC (Greater Beloit Economic
    Development Corporation)
    example, 81
Goals, 27–31, 33, 39–40, 70, 72
"Golden circles," 11
Goldsmith, Marshall, 21
"Good enough" concept as
    barrier, 105
Good to Great (Collins), 63
Greater Beloit Economic
    Development Corporation
    (GBEDC) example, 81
Green Bay Packers example, 92–93
Greenberg, Cathy, 21
Guest Speaker activities, 118–119

Hassel, Emily, 75
Hattie, John, 15, 72–73
Henderson, Anne, 82–83
*High Quality Professional
    Development for Teachers*
    (DelMonte), 75–76
Hollengzer, Lara, 95
Hubbell, E., 15
Hu-Chan, Maya, 21

Implementation, 40–41, 92–95
Individualization, 66–67
Innovation Schools, 99
INSPIRE project, 37
Institute for Community Research, 4
Integration, 77–80, 110–111
Intentionality, 65–66
International High School
    example, 73
Interstate Teacher Assessment and
    Support Consortium
    standards, 111

Jacobson, R., 22
Joint instruction stage of
    relationships, 8

Kellogg Company partnership,
    99–100
Kermis festival example, 74–75
Kolb, David, 2–3, 12

Leadership
    distributive, 89–91
    lollipop moments, 85–86
    mindful, 91–92
    need for, 85–86
    risk tolerance of, 86–88
    situational, 88–89
    systems implementation and, 92–95
    toxicity of, 103–104
Leading in a Culture of Change
    (Fullan), 104
Learning process
    goals, 27–28, 29
    levels in community-based
        learning, 6–9
    theories, 12–13
    See also Curriculum; Framework
        of community-based learning
Lewin, K., 12
Literacy standards, 115–116
Lollipop moments, 85–86

Mann, David, 40
Manor New Tech High School, 4–5
Map activities, 37–39, 38 (figure),
    117–120
Mapp, Karen, 82–83
Marzano, Robert, 13, 82
Mathews, David, 18, 64
Mayer-Mihalski, N., 101
McTighe, J., 42, 67
Mediocrity, 40–41
Meetings, 58, 91
Melaville, A., 22
Mindful leadership, 91–92
Mission statements, 74
Moreno, Jacob, 38
Multipliers (Wiseman), 103

Naches Valley Intermediate School
    example, 65
National Alliance for School Reform
    (NASR), 79
Negative partners, 41
Neighborhood Study sample,
    115–120
No Child Left Behind, 76

Orentlicher, David, 22
Orvis, Bob, 89

Partnerships
    assessing, 67–70, 68 (table),
        69 (table)
    barriers in, 102
    connections needed for, 64
    learning levels of, 7–9
    mapping, 37–39, 38 (figure)
    Neighborhood Study
        example, 120
    planning for, 77
    pyramid of levels, 7, 37
    South High School example, 54
    tracking spreadsheets for,
        39 (table)
    See also specific partners
Passion, 34
Piaget, Jean, 12
Pietersen, W., 105
Pitler, H., 15
Place-based learning, 5–6, 18
Planning process, 28–33
    See also Sustainability plans
Polka music example, 66
Practices
    championing, 64–65
    customization and
        individualization, 66–67
    evaluating partnerships, 67–70,
        68 (table), 69 (table)
    intentional focus, 65–66
    "knocking it out of the park,"
        62–63
    observing potential transfers, 66
    staff selection, 63–64
PreK-18 councils, 42
Pretest activity, 117
Principals, 101, 111–112
Professional development
    best practices, 72–75
    establishing student goals, 72
    knowledge and skills, 80–82
    resource identification, 75–77
    teacher options, 77–80

Professional preparation programs,
    12–13
Project-based learning, 5, 14
Pyramid, partnership, 7, 37

Raveling, George, 109
Reflection, 27–28, 41, 82
Relationships, 7–9
    See also Partnerships
Relevance, 2–3, 9
Research, 80
Resource identification, 75–77
Responsibility assignments, 26–27
Risk tolerance/aversion, 86–88,
    100–102
River studies example, 90
Robertson, Alastair, 21
Role assignments, 26–27
Rubrics, 44–46 (figure)

Sanders, Mavis, 95
Scale-up process, 36–37, 39, 67–70,
    79–80
Schlechty, Phil, 2
Schneider, E. Joseph, 95
School improvement, 39–40
School visits, 82
Science standards, 116–117
Senge, Peter, 42, 74
Service learning, 6
Sinek, Simon, 11–12
Situational leadership, 88–89
SMART goals, 39–40
Sobel, David, 18
Social nature of instruction, 13–16
Social studies standards, 116
Sociograms, 38
South High School example
    background, 50–52
    challenges, 53–55
    exceeding expectations, 57–59
    progress, 52–53
    setbacks, 56–57
Stanford-Blair, Nancy, 14
Stein Rogan and Partners, 17
Stone, B.J., 15

Student engagement, 2, 4–5, 54–56, 58
Student rubrics, 46 (figure)
Superintendents, 112–113
Sustainability plans
  about, 33–34
  partnership mapping, 37–39, 38 (figure)
  passion, 34
  school improvement from, 39–40
  three-month legacies, 35–36

Target stores example, 12–13
Teachers. *See* Curriculum; Educators; Professional development
Technology, 120
3-2-1 Bridge activity, 117
Three-month legacies, 35–36
Time as barrier, 98–100, 103
Timperly, Helen, 80
Toxic leaders, 103–104
Transfers, 66
Trust, 92
Two Presidents Are Better Than One (Orentlicher), 22

Unified School District. *See* South High School example
Unintentional benchmarks, 27, 117
University partnerships, 99–100

Vars, G., 78–79
Visional representations. *See* Dashboards
Vision setting, 22–26, 74
Vollmer, Jamie, 3, 9, 17, 18, 74
Vygotsky, Lev, 15

Waiting process as barrier, 103
"Wants over needs" concept as barrier, 106–107
Webb, Norman L., 13
Whistle language example, 66
"Why Countries Go to War" example, 43, 47
Wiggins, G. P., 42, 67
Window cleaning analogy, 106–107
Wiseman, Liz, 103
Woodbridge State High School example, 65

A SAGE Company

Corwin is committed to improving education for all learners by publishing books and other professional development resources for those serving the field of PreK–12 education. By providing practical, hands-on materials, Corwin continues to carry out the promise of its motto: **"Helping Educators Do Their Work Better."**